5
Christ Our Life

We Worship

AUTHORS

Sisters of Notre Dame of Chardon, Ohio
Sister Mary Theresa Betz, S.N.D.
Sister Mary St. Leo DeChant, S.N.D.
Sister Mary Kathleen Glavich, S.N.D.
Sister Mary Ann Hvizda, S.N.D.
Sister Mary Verne Kavula, S.N.D.
Sister Mary Patricia Lab, S.N.D.
Sister Mary Andrew Miller, S.N.D.
Sister Mary Jean Strathern, S.N.D.

THEOLOGICAL ADVISOR

Sister Agnes Cunningham, S.S.C.M.

CONSULTANTS

Joseph Martos
The Reverend Lawrence E. Mick

GENERAL EDITOR

Sister Mary Kathleen Glavich, S.N.D.

LOYOLAPRESS.

CHICAGO

Nihil Obstat: The Reverend Robert J. Kropac, S.T.B., Censor Deputatus
Imprimatur: The Most Reverend Anthony M. Pilla, D.D., M.A., Bishop of Cleveland
Given at Cleveland, Ohio, on 6 May 1996

The *Nihil Obstat* and *Imprimatur* are official declarations that a book or pamphlet is free of doctrinal or moral error. No implication is contained therein that those who have granted the *Nihil Obstat* and *Imprimatur* agree with the contents, opinions, or statements expressed.

Christ Our Life
found to be in conformity

The Ad Hoc Committee to Oversee the Use of the Catechism, National Conference of Catholic Bishops, has found this catechetical series, copyright 1997 and 2002, to be in conformity with the *Catechism of the Catholic Church*.

Dedicated to St. Julie Billiart, foundress of the Sisters of Notre Dame, in gratitude for her inspiration and example

Acknowledgments

This present revision of the Christ Our Life series is the work of countless people. In particular, we acknowledge and thank the following for their roles in the project:

- The Sisters of Notre Dame who supported the production of the Christ Our Life series, especially Sister Mary Joell Overman, S.N.D.; Sister Mary Frances Murray, S.N.D.; and Sister Mary Margaret Hess, S.N.D.
- The Sisters of Notre Dame and others who over the past twenty years have shaped, written, and edited editions of the Christ Our Life series, in particular Sister Mary de Angelis Bothwell, S.N.D., the former editor
- Those who worked on different stages involved in producing this edition, especially Sister Mary Julie Boehnlein, S.N.D.; Sister Linda Marie Gecewicz, S.N.D.; Sister Mary Beth Gray, S.N.D.; Sister Joanmarie Harks, S.N.D.; Sister Mary Nanette Herman, S.N.D.; Sister Mary Andrew Miller, S.N.D.; Sister Mary Agnes O'Malley, S.N.D.; Sister Mary Catherine Rennecker, S.N.D.; and Sister Mary St. Jude Weisensell, S.N.D.
- Those catechists, directors of religious education, priests, parents, students, and others who responded to surveys, returned evaluation forms, wrote letters, or participated in interviews to help improve the series

Scripture selections are taken from The New American Bible, Copyright © 1991, 1986, 1970 by the Confraternity of Christian Doctrine, Washington, D.C., and are used by license of the copyright owner. All rights reserved.

Excerpts from the English translation of *Rite of Marriage* © 1969, International Committee on English in the Liturgy, Inc. (ICEL); excerpts from the English translation of *Rite of Baptism for Children* © 1969, ICEL; excerpts from the English translation of *Lectionary for Mass* © 1969, 1981, ICEL; excerpts from the English translation of *The Roman Missal* © 1973, International Committee on English in the Liturgy, Inc. (ICEL); excerpts from the English translation of *Rite of Penance* © 1974, ICEL; excerpts from the English translation of *Rite of Confirmation (2nd edition)* © 1975, ICEL; excerpts from the English translation of *The Ordination of Deacons, Priests, and Bishops* © 1975, ICEL; excerpts from the English translation of *Pastoral Care of the Sick* © 1982, ICEL; excerpts from the English translation of *A Book of Prayers* © 1982, ICEL; excerpts from the English translation of *Book of Blessings* © 1988, ICEL. All rights reserved.

Concordat cum originali: Ronald F. Krisman, Executive Director, Secretariat for the Liturgy, National Conference of Catholic Bishops

Text of the Apostles' Creed and the Nicene Creed by the International Consultation on English Texts.

Excerpt from *The Ways of Prayer* by Michael Pennock © 1987 by Ave Maria Press, Notre Dame, Indiana. Used by permission.

Additional information for Family Feature pages 42A–D was provided by the Mexican Fine Arts Center Museum, Chicago, Illinois.

All attempts possible have been made to contact publisher for cited works in this book.

Photographs

© **Archive Photos** (p. 118); © **Tony Arruza** (p. 29); © **Dave Bartruff/CORBIS** (p. 3 top); © **Catholic News Service** (p. 26); © **Cleo Freelance Photography** (p. 152 top); © **Corbis Corp.** (pp. 99, 138, 140A, 151); © **Corel Corporation** (pp. 84, 89); © **Paul Dancel/Tony Stone Worldwide** (p. 122); © **Digital Stock Corp.** (pp. 97 bottom left, 111, 157); © **Amy C. Etra/PhotoEdit** (p. 31); © **EyeWire** (pp. 113, 163); © **Myrleen Ferguson/PhotoEdit** (pp. 4, 91 top, 152 bottom, 179, 193); © **David Hiser/Tony Stone Images** (p. 74); © **Brent Jones** (p. 178A); © **Kids for Saving Earth** (p. 148); © **Alan Oddie/PhotoEdit** (p. 144 bottom); © **PhotoDisc, Inc.** (pp. 2, 5, 15, 44, 46, 52, 65, 90, 97 top left and right, 101, 110A, 112, 124, 141, 170, 186, 192); © **Eugene D. Plaisted, O.S.C./Crosiers** (pp. i, iii, 8, 21, 28, 39, 59, 80A, 81, 117, 135, 176, 178C, 184 top, 190–191); © **Leonard de Selva/CORBIS** (p. 75); © **James L. Shaffer** (pp. 48, 49 top, 55, 60, 61, 67, 68, 72, 130); © **Skjold Photographs** (pp. 123, 145 right, 172, 184 bottom); © **SuperStock, Inc.** (pp. 3 bottom, 85); © **VCG/FPG International LLC.** (p. 121); © **Wheater/Maryknoll Missioners** (p. 24 bottom); © **W. P. Wittman Limited** (pp. 1, 10, 16–17, 18 left, 22, 24 top, 43, 45, 49 bottom, 55, 69, 91 bottom, 92, 96, 98, 125, 128–129, 132–133, 145 left, 183).

Artwork

Lois Axeman (p. 146); **Jeff Busch** (p. 33); **Don Dyen** (pp. 71, 82, 106, 115); **Lydia Halverson** (pp. 87, 88, 102); **George Hamblin/Steven Edsey & Sons** (pp. 42A–C); **Barry Kafka** (p. 214); **Laser Type and Graphics** (p. 101); **Diana Magnuson** (pp. 136, 137, 158); **Robert Masheris** (pp. 53, 66, 120); **Dick Mlodock** (pp. 171, 173, 180, 182); **Mike Muir** (pp. 8, 11 left, 34, 62); **Mary O'Connor** (p. 98); **Proof Positive/Farrowlyne Assoc., Inc.** (pp. 12, 16, 18, 27 top, 35, 38, 50, 63, 73, 80, 94, 110C–D, 122, 126, 140B–D, 167, 189); **Robert Voigts** (rites boxes pp. 48, 52, 58, 71, commandment boxes pp. 143, 150, 151, 156, 157, 164, pp. 6, 11 right, 13, 15, 19–20, 24, 25, 27 bottom, 30, 36, 37, 40–41, 47, 54–58, 61, 72, 76–78, 83, 90, 95, 103–104, 108–110, 112, 114, 127, 131, 134, 138–140, 148, 153–155, 162, 164, 165, 169, 174, 175, 182, 183, 184, 187, 194, 211, 213, 218, 219, 221, 223, 225); **Mike Watson** (pp. 142, 224); **Mary Wilshire** (pp. 156, 166).

Cover design by Donald Kye.
Cover Art © Eugene D. Plaisted, O.S.C./Crosiers.

06 07 DBH 7 6

LOYOLAPRESS.

3441 N. Ashland Avenue
Chicago, Illinois 60657
(800) 621-1008

CONTENTS

5

CONTENTS

5

Things Every Catholic Should Know

The Ten Commandments
1. I, the Lord, am your God. You shall not have other gods besides me.
2. You shall not take the name of the Lord, your God, in vain.
3. Remember to keep holy the Sabbath day.
4. Honor your father and your mother.
5. You shall not kill.
6. You shall not commit adultery.
7. You shall not steal.
8. You shall not bear false witness against your neighbor.
9. You shall not covet your neighbor's wife.
10. You shall not covet anything that belongs to your neighbor.

Holy Days of Obligation in the United States
Solemnity of Mary, Mother of God: *January 1*
We honor Mary, Mother of God.

Ascension: *Fortieth day after Easter*
Jesus ascended into heaven.

Assumption: *August 15*
Mary was taken into heaven, body and soul.

All Saints' Day: *November 1*
We honor all the saints in heaven.

Immaculate Conception: *December 8*
Mary was free from sin from the first moment of her life.

Christmas: *December 25*
We celebrate the birth of Jesus.

The Seven Sacraments
Baptism, Confirmation, Eucharist, Reconciliation (Penance), Anointing of the Sick, Matrimony, Holy Orders

Corporal Works of Mercy
Feed the hungry
Give drink to the thirsty
Clothe the naked
Visit the sick
Shelter the homeless
Visit the imprisoned
Bury the dead

Spiritual Works of Mercy
Warn the sinner
Instruct the ignorant
Counsel the doubtful
Comfort the sorrowing
Bear wrongs patiently
Forgive all injuries
Pray for the living and the dead

The Mysteries of the Rosary
Joyful Mysteries
The Annunciation
The Visitation
The Nativity
The Presentation in the Temple
The Finding of Jesus in the Temple

Sorrowful Mysteries
The Agony in the Garden
The Scourging at the Pillar
The Crowning with Thorns
The Carrying of the Cross
The Crucifixion and Death of Jesus

Glorious Mysteries
The Resurrection
The Ascension
The Descent of the Holy Spirit
The Assumption of Mary
The Crowning of Mary as Queen of Heaven and Earth

Notes to Parents

Goal of This Year's Program

This year your child will be learning the meaning of worshiping God in community. The worship of God includes prayer and service. We give worship to God through the celebration of the Eucharist and all the sacraments. These are described as liturgy, which is the Church's official public worship. Through a study of liturgy, the children become aware of Christ's work of salvation. They learn to participate more fully in order to give thanks and praise to God.

A Family Program

Because your faith makes a profound impact on your child, a parent page is provided on blackline masters for each unit of We Worship.

The pages are designed to help your family pray together and to give you an understanding of the goals and message of each unit. Each page contains the following four sections.

The Church Speaks

A quotation from a recent Church document states concisely the "changeless mystery of our faith" that forms the basis for the doctrine taught in each unit.

Reflecting on the Message

The excerpt in "The Church Speaks" is elaborated on to give you an explanation of the content of the unit.

Growing in Christ's Love

Prayers and activities related to the unit your child is currently studying are suggested to enhance your spiritual growth.

Worship and Your Family

To foster an atmosphere of love in your home, use the activities suggested that are most relevant to your family. Witnessing Christ acting in your family as you grow in love of God and of one another will be a rewarding experience.

Family Feature

Each of the units in this book ends with four Family Feature pages that suggest family customs and provide review activities.

Celebrating with Your Family

At the end of each unit you may receive a sheet that provides ideas for a family celebration. The suggested celebration combines knowledge, the doctrine of the faith, with good works, the witness of faith, and prayer, the heart of faith.

Other Means for Family Involvement

Besides using the parent pages, the Family Feature pages, and the family celebrations, you can help your child in the following ways:

- Encourage your child to memorize Things Every Catholic Should Know, found on page v.

- Help your child carry out some of the activities in the Things to Do at Home section at the end of each chapter.

Help your child master the content in the We Remember section at the end of each chapter.

We Worship God as Catholic Christians

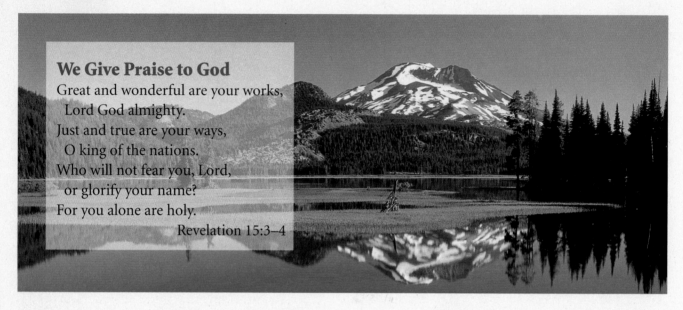

We Give Praise to God
Great and wonderful are your works,
  Lord God almighty.
Just and true are your ways,
  O king of the nations.
Who will not fear you, Lord,
  or glorify your name?
For you alone are holy.
                    Revelation 15:3–4

Check the experiences that you have had.

❏ Flying in a plane and seeing the world
  below
❏ Being in a wide-open space at night and
  looking up at a million bright stars
❏ Waking up and feeling good with the sun
  streaming in the window
❏ Knowing there is someone who loves you
  very much
❏ Standing overlooking a lovely waterfall
❏ Holding a newborn baby and noticing his
  or her tiny fingernails and delicate
  eyelashes
❏ Hearing very beautiful, moving music

Recall how you felt during these experiences. Write your feelings here.

_____

_____

_____

The wonders of the world and the joys of being alive lead us to praise or adore God. God is the all-powerful One who created the universe. God is the all-loving One who gives us life. When we realize God's greatness and God's gifts, our hearts fill with admiration and thanks. Sometimes we want to shout with joy to God. We want to give God glory because he is great and good and has done wonderful things.

Men and women who do great things become our heroes and heroines. We honor them with awards, words of praise, gifts, and celebrations. We honor God with **worship.**

Lord, one more
day to love you!
—Charles de Foucauld

All Are Called to Worship

In all countries and periods of time people have believed in a god or gods. They have built grand temples and monuments. They have held long, colorful ceremonies, and they have prayed and chanted praise. They have offered **sacrifices,** or gifts, in worship: their possessions, their animals, and sometimes even their lives.

The one true God wants everyone to live with him in love, but he chose the people of Israel as his special people. God revealed himself to the Israelites and taught them to worship him. The Israelites responded to God's love. They offered sacrifices to God in the temple. Families set aside a place of prayer in their homes. In their buildings of prayer, called **synagogues,** they praised and thanked God for all he had done for them. They listened to God's Word in the Sacred Scriptures.

Christian worship grew out of Jewish worship. The first Christians worshiped as Jesus had taught them. They prayed together in the temple every day. They prayed the

Jews
↓

Our Father that they had learned from Jesus. But their greatest act of worship was the **Eucharist.** Through this sacred meal they thanked God with Jesus for all he had done for them. They offered themselves, with Jesus, to the Father.

Many people do not know the true God. They do not know that Jesus is the way to the Father. But all people are sons or daughters of God. All people are called to worship God. We can help lead them to Jesus by our prayers and our love, by talking to them, and by supporting missionaries.

How wonderful it is to belong to God! He made us, and we are his people. God's love for us is everlasting. We love and honor him above everything and everyone. We worship him. Worship is our way of telling God that we know we belong to him.

We worship God when we pray. In prayer we adore God as the perfect One who created us. We ask him as our Savior to forgive us. We ask him as the Holy Spirit to make us holy. We thank God for all he gives to us.

Sometimes we pray together with other people in God's family. At other times we pray alone. We talk to God and give him time to talk to us. God lets us come to know him when we pray. Every day God has new things to share with us.

Everything God has made tells us something about his great power and love, but we often miss the message. We need to take time to think quietly about God's greatness. Then we will want to cry out **Alleluia!** *Alleluia* is

from the Hebrew for "praise God." (*Hallel* means "praise," and *yah* is the first syllable of *Yahweh*, "God.")

Think how great and good God is. Check the ways you will give him praise.

___✓___ By praying every morning and evening
___✓___ By taking time to see the beauty in creation
___✓___ By being quiet long enough to hear God speak in my heart
_____ By talking with God about what happens each day
___✓___ By often repeating short prayers such as "My God, I love you."

What else will you do to show God you want to praise him? Write it here.

going to church

_____

We Worship through Prayer

Come, let us sing joyfully to the LORD;
    cry out to the rock of our salvation.
Let us greet him with a song of praise,
    joyfully sing out our psalms.
For the LORD is the great God,
    the great king over all gods,
Whose hand holds the depths of the earth;
    who owns the tops of the mountains.
The sea and dry land belong to God,
    who made them, formed them by hand.

Enter, let us bow down in worship;
    let us kneel before the LORD who made us.
Psalm 95:1–6

and often cared for them himself. After morning Mass, King Louis would ride his horse through towns in his kingdom. He wanted to see for himself how the people were treated by the powerful nobles. He listened to their complaints. King Louis passed laws to protect the poor and weak. He made the nobles give back what they had taken from the poor.

We Worship through Service

We worship God by our good deeds, too. When we treat everyone and everything with love and respect, we give honor to God. We worship him by the loving service we give to others. How are the people in the pictures giving loving service?

Take time to think about how you can worship God when you

✢ are eating lunch,
✢ are riding the bus to school,
✢ are asked to turn off the television set,
✢ get something your brothers and sisters or friends don't have, and
✢ see someone who needs help.

St. Louis, King of France, Was a True Worshiper

Twelve-year-old Louis IX was named king of France in 1226, when his father died. His mother ruled until he was twenty-one. Under her guidance Louis became a just and courageous king. The night before he was crowned, Louis fasted and prayed in order to prepare himself to be God's servant, a good and holy king.

During his reign King Louis had many churches and hospitals constructed. He was merciful to rebels and worked for peace. Louis also tried to bring justice to the poor. He saw to it that food and clothing were given to the needy. The king visited the sick

During war Louis shared the hardships of his soldiers, taking no privileges. Once Louis was captured. Even in prison he prayed the Liturgy of the Hours every day.

When Louis was dying, he prayed the psalm verse "Lord, I will enter into your house. I will worship in your holy temple, and will give glory to your name." Through his prayer, his support of the Church, and his Christlike service to all, St. Louis had made his whole life an act of worship.

Things to Do at Home

1. Find Psalm 148 in your family Bible and read it. Give your family time to think about it. Then add your own prayers of praise.
2. Ask everyone in the family to name some things people around the world say and do to worship God. Write down at least five of the answers.
3. Collect five prayers of praise. Ask people for ideas, look in prayer books or in the Book of Psalms, or make up your own.
4. Memorize Psalm 95.
5. Invite someone to go with you to Sunday Mass.

We Remember

Why do we worship God?
We worship God because he is great and good and because we belong to him. We love and honor God above all else.

How do we worship God?
We worship God through prayer, loving service, and sacrifice.

Words to Know

worship	alleluia	sacrifice
Eucharist	synagogue	

We Respond

Show yourself over the heavens, God;
may your glory appear above all
the earth.

Psalm 57:12

We Review

Ways to Worship Read the statements below and fill in the missing letters. Letters from the word *worship* have been inserted to give you clues.

W 1. When we honor God above everything, we w _o r s h i p_ him.

O 2. We kneel as a sign that we _a d_ o _r e_ God.

R 3. When we speak of God's greatness and goodness, we _p_ r _a i s e_ him.

S 4. Our good deeds of loving s _e r v e n t_ worship God.

H 5. The greatest act of worship is the _E u c_ h _a r i s t_.

I 6. We worship by offering God a _s a c_ r i _f i c e_.

P 7. We give worship to God when we p _r a y_.

God, Our Greatest Hero   St. Francis of Assisi composed a prayer praising God for the sun, the moon, and the stars, for wind, water, fire, and earth. Think of five reasons you want to praise God. List them here. Then make them into a prayer.

1. I f thank God for my family
2. I thank God for friends
3. I thank God for air light
4. I thank God for for rain
5. I thank Go God for my brain

Dear God I thank you for all things that is good I also want to thank you for my family, friends, air, light, rain, and my brain Amen.

Jesus Calls Us to Worship with Him

2

Jesus Offered Perfect Worship to the Father

In the story of Pinocchio, Gepetto, a lonely woodcarver, makes a puppet of a little boy. Loving the boy he carved out of wood, Gepetto wishes it were real with all his heart. Lo and behold, one night the puppet, Pinocchio, comes to life. Then he becomes like a son to Gepetto.

Our story is like Pinocchio's! God, our creator, loved us so much that he wanted us to share his divine life. Now we are able to enjoy a life greater than our human life. This share in God's life is called **grace.**

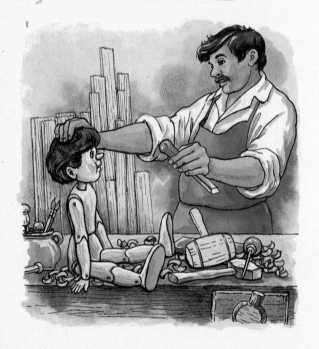

Jesus Christ, the Son of God, made grace possible for us. He became human like us to redeem us. He lived, suffered, died, and rose to save us from the power of sin and death. He invites us to share his life.

Jesus offered the Father all the words and actions of his life. Jesus loved his Father and was happy to give him glory. He worshiped the Father through perfect prayer and loving service to others. Finally, he offered the greatest act of worship: he sacrificed himself on the cross on Calvary.

Through the grace received in Baptism we are made like Christ. We are able to worship the Father with him. Jesus calls us to join him in *prayer, loving service,* and *sacrifice.* The more closely we follow Jesus, the more we grow in grace and the more we are united with him.

We can learn from the Gospels of Matthew, Mark, Luke, and John how Jesus worshiped the Father. The word *gospel* means "good news." The Gospels are the written Good News that Jesus saved us from sin and death.

Some examples of how Jesus worshiped are told in Mark 1:35–39. *Mark 1:35–39* is a Scripture reference. It means

Mark	**1**	**35–39**
(name of book)	(chapter)	(verses)

and is read "Mark, chapter one, verses thirty-five through thirty-nine." Practice reading these:

Luke 19:1–10   2 Corinthians 4:7–12
Genesis 2:5–7   Mark 15:42–16:8
Romans 11:33–36

Read Mark 1:35–39 in the box on this page. Find things Jesus did to worship the Father. List them.

He prayed to God. ~~He is preaching~~
He preached in the synagues
He drove out demons

Jesus Leaves Capernaum.

[35]Rising very early before dawn, he left and went off to a deserted place, where he prayed. [36]Simon and those who were with him pursued him [37]and on finding him said, "Everyone is looking for you." [38]He told them, "Let us go on to the nearby villages that I may preach there also. For this purpose have I come." [39]So he went into their synagogues, preaching and driving out demons throughout the whole of Galilee.

Use the New Testament to look up and read these references. How did Jesus worship the Father in each event? Write your answer on the line.

Matthew 26:36 ~~He prayed~~ praying

Mark 1:29–31 healing

Luke 4:31–32 teaching people

John 19:29–30 ~~dea dejying~~ on the cross

We Can Worship Like Jesus

Match each of Jesus' acts of worship with a way that you can imitate it from the second column.

Jesus Worships

1. ___D___ He obeys his Father in all things.

2. ___F___ He prays alone.

3. ___B___ He heals the sick.

4. ___H___ He spreads the Good News.

5. ___A___ He prays with the Jewish people in the synagogue.

6. ___G___ He cares for people's needs.

7. ___C___ He forgives sins.

8. ___E___ He dies on the cross.

I Worship

A. I participate in Mass.

B. I send a card to a friend in the hospital.

C. I accept someone's apology and do not hold a grudge.

D. I do what my parents tell me even when I do not understand.

E. I do something very hard and offer it for an intention.

F. I find quiet time to pray each day.

G. I cheer up someone who is sad.

H. I tell someone what I learned in religion class.

Prayerfully reading the Gospels helps you to be a true Christian:

- Slowly read a passage in the Gospels to see how Jesus lived.
- Reflect on how you can model your life on him.
- Pray to God dwelling within you for strength and courage to imitate the life Jesus lived on earth.

Jesus Shows Us the Father's Love

Jesus came to earth to show us the Father's love and to save us. We read in Scripture that he did many wonderful things for people who came to him with faith:

✤ offered them life
✤ laid hands upon them
✤ fed them
✤ forgave their sins and spoke words of peace and cured them
✤ blessed a couple by coming to their wedding
✤ invited some people to be his special followers.

Finally, Jesus showed the depth of God's love for us when he died on the cross and rose to new life.

Today Jesus is still at work in the world. Through his Church he continues to save us. Through the sacraments he cares for our special needs.

The **sacraments** are sacred signs in which we meet Jesus and receive from him a share in God's life. The Eastern Catholic Church calls the sacraments *mysteries.* They are actions of Jesus and his Church. Catholics celebrate seven sacraments.

Sacraments of Initiation
Baptism, Confirmation, Eucharist

Sacraments of Healing
Reconciliation, Anointing of the Sick

Sacraments of Vocation
Marriage, Holy Orders

We are surrounded by signs. We communicate with others by signs. All signs give us a message. What do these signs say?

The sacraments are celebrations. What words or actions are related to the following celebrations?

a birthday _~~and playing games~~ blowing can dle_

singing Happy Birthday

Independence Day _fireworks party_
~~picnic~~ _wave our flag_

graduation _~~see~~ geting awards have a party say ~~congrats~~ congrats_

Christmas _geting gifts, put up ~~Chrisla~~ Christmas tree sing Christmas songs, go to mass_

Through the years we continue to use these words and actions for these celebrations. They are signs that have meaning for us.

The words and actions of each sacrament are special signs. Through them Jesus not only shows what he is doing for us but offers us his grace. We call these words and actions the **rite** of the sacrament. In the rite, certain objects are used as signs of the special grace that is offered in each sacrament. Some of the objects used are water, oil, bread, and wine.

In *faith* we believe that Jesus comes to us and gives us special gifts or graces in the sacraments. Each time we celebrate one of the sacraments, our faith grows stronger. We grow closer to Jesus, and he makes us holier through the Holy Spirit. The whole Church also grows in holiness.

The sacraments are a part of the Church's **liturgy,** or public worship. The Mass and the prayers of the Church that are called the **Liturgy of the Hours** (or Divine Office) are also part of the liturgy. Through them we give public worship to God.

As you go through this book, you will study each of the sacraments. You will learn how Christ and the Church show us God's love through the sacraments. Whenever we celebrate them in faith, we grow in love of God. We thank God and give him joyful praise!

Things to Do at Home

1. How many sacraments have the members of your family celebrated? List them.
2. Make flashcards of these words: *grace*, *rite*, *liturgy*, and *sacraments*.
3. Do one thing this evening that will make you more like Christ.
4. Write a poem about worship.

We Remember

How did Jesus worship the Father?
Jesus worshiped the Father through prayer, loving service, and sacrifice.

What is liturgy?
Liturgy is the public worship of the Church. It includes the sacraments, especially the Eucharist, and the Liturgy of the Hours.

We Respond

Jesus, help me celebrate the sacraments with faith and act the way you would act.

We Review

An Acrostic   Use the clues to fill in the blanks.

1. G o s p e l s
2. w o r s h i p
3. f a i t h
4. S a c r a m e n t
5. r i t e s

1. The written accounts of the life of Jesus
2. Prayer and service to God
3. What we need to celebrate a sacrament and what grows each time we celebrate a sacrament
4. Sacred sign in which we meet Jesus and receive God's life
5. The words and actions of the sacraments

If your answers are correct, the letters in the boxes spell what Jesus made possible for us by his life, death, and resurrection. Write it here:

_____

_____

Seven Lifelines to Heaven Fill in the missing words. Use the words in the frame to help you.

actions   graces

signs

holy

1. Sacraments are _signs_ in which we meet Jesus.

2. In the sacraments, Jesus shares God's _life_ with us.

3. Jesus shows us what he is doing for us through the words

   and _actions_ of each sacrament.

4. When we come to the sacraments with faith, Jesus offers us

   special _graces_ .

5. Through the sacraments, Jesus makes us _holy_ .

6. In the sacraments, the whole Church gives _worship_ to God.

7. The sacraments are part of the Church's _liturgy_ .

8. The liturgy is the _public_ worship of the Church.

worship

life

liturgy   public

flood   *rain*   *life*   *river*   *drink*

Baptism Is a Celebration of Life

What comes to your mind when you think of water? In each drop write a word related to water.

What would happen to us if we had no water to drink? We would not live very long. What would happen if there were no water for the grass, trees, and flowers? Nothing would grow, and the earth would become a desert. Without water, life would soon come to an end.

Water produces life and growth, which is one reason water is a good sign for the Sacrament of Baptism. Water reminds us of the wonderful new life of grace God gives us in Baptism. Through the Paschal Mystery, Baptism makes us adopted children of God and members of Jesus' family, the Church. The Trinity dwells in us, and the gifts of the Holy Spirit help us become like Jesus. Water reminds us of our growing friendship with God.

Besides bringing forth life, water cleanses. Baptism cleanses us from the **original sin** we were born with as members of the human race. It also cleanses us from any sins we have committed.

Water in the form of storms and floods can also bring death. This makes water an even

more powerful sign for Baptism, for in Baptism we enter into the death and rising of Jesus. We promise to die to sin and rise to new life in Christ. Dying and rising is a pattern throughout life. We say good-bye to the old and meet the new. We suffer and come out stronger, better persons. Most important, over and over we turn from sin to new life. This change from the death of sin to life is called **conversion.**

Baptism is the first sacrament we celebrate. Jesus taught how necessary it is: "No one can enter the kingdom of God without being born of water and Spirit" (John 3:5). Baptism marks us forever as Christians, committed to spreading God's kingdom.

Baptism Initiates Us

Adults who wish to belong to the Catholic Church enter a special program. It is called the **Rite of Christian Initiation of Adults (RCIA).** People who are in the RCIA are called **catechumens.** In the RCIA catechumens learn about the Catholic faith. The Catholic community helps them experience Catholic life, worship, and ministry. They decide whether or not they want to convert their lives and become new persons in Christ. Then, usually during the Easter Vigil, they celebrate the three sacraments of initiation: Baptism, Confirmation, and the Eucharist. With the other members of the Catholic Church, they declare their belief in Jesus and his teachings. They are called to love God and others as Jesus did. They are subject to Church laws. They are invited to worship God with Jesus in prayer and service. Together they can celebrate Jesus' love in the sacraments, especially in the Eucharist.

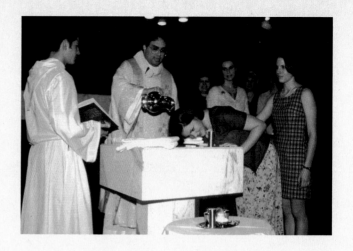

You, though, probably were welcomed into the faith community as a baby. At your Baptism, your parents and godparents promised to share their faith with you. They promised to help you live as a good Christian. Because you received new life when you were baptized, the day of your Baptism is your birthday as a Christian. It is a day to remember and celebrate.

MY BIRTHDAY AS A CHRISTIAN

Fill in the information.

I became a member of my human family on the day of my birth.

My family name is ___Wm_____ .

I became a member of God's family at my Baptism.

The name I received at Baptism is _____ .

The day I was born to new life with Christ was ___2/12_____ .

My godparents were _____ .

The priest or deacon who baptized me was _____ .

The church where I was baptized was _____ Church.

The Christian Community Celebrates Baptism

The baptismal rites for adults, for older children, and for infants are similar. The steps and symbols of the rite of infant baptism are explained here.

When new friends come to visit, we introduce them to our family. We try to make them feel welcome. When infants are brought to be baptized, the priest or deacon calls them by name. He welcomes them to the Christian community with joy. In its name he claims them for Christ by tracing the **Sign of the Cross** on their foreheads. Then he invites the parents and godparents to do the same. This reminds the parents that Jesus saved us by the cross and that their child belongs to God. It reminds them to help their child live as a child of God.

The Bible tells us about the Christian life. At a baptism the priest or deacon reads from **Scripture.** Then he explains the readings and the meaning of Baptism.

Next, everyone prays for those who are to be baptized and says a litany of the saints. The priest or deacon prays that the infants will be freed from sin and strengthened against evil. The infants are anointed with **oil** and brought to the baptismal font.

As the priest or deacon blesses the water, he mentions the wonderful ways God has used water. The prayer recalls that Baptism gives us a share in Jesus' death and resurrection.

We ask you, Father, with your Son, to send the Holy Spirit upon the water of this font. May all who are buried with Christ in the death of baptism rise also with him to newness of life. (We ask this) through our Lord. Amen.

Then the parents and godparents tell everyone present that they reject Satan and his ways. They profess their faith in Christ Jesus and in his Church. They tell the priest or deacon that they want their child to be baptized in this same faith.

A Child Is Baptized

In Baptism, the priest or deacon calls the child by name and says,

> I baptize you in the name of the Father, and of the Son, and of the Holy Spirit.

As he says this, three times he pours the sacred water over the infant, or lowers the infant into the water. The words and the water are the signs that bring about new life in Christ. After Baptism the new member of the Church is anointed with **chrism,** an oil blessed by the bishop. This is a sign that the baptized is a member of God's family. The child may now share in Christian worship.

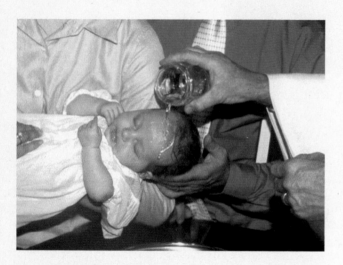

A **white garment** is then put on the newly baptized. It is a sign that the child has been clothed in Christ. The family and friends are reminded that their example should help the newly baptized live free from sin.

A **candle** lighted from the Easter candle is *Paschal* given to the family. It is a reminder that in Baptism we receive the light of Christ. The parents and godparents are told to keep the light burning brightly. They must help their child walk always as a child of God. They must help him or her keep the flame of faith alive. Then, when the Lord comes, their child will be ready to meet him with all the saints.

At the end of the celebration, everyone prays the Our Father. Then a blessing is prayed for the mother, the father, and everyone present.

Baptism Is Lived

Through Baptism we become new people in Christ. We "put on" the Lord Jesus. We are to live as God's children by keeping away from sin and by living Christ's way of love.

The sign of a Christian is love. Draw a picture of yourself doing something that shows your love.

Sacramentals Help Us

Every time we bless ourselves with holy water, we are reminded of our new life in Christ. We remember that Jesus is with us. Holy water is a sacramental. So is the Sign of the Cross. **Sacramentals** are words, actions, and objects blessed by the Church that bring us closer to God. How much they help us depends on the way we use them.

Circle any of the sacramentals that have helped you live as a Christian.

Words to Know

original sin	catechumen
conversion	chrism
RCIA	sacramentals

Words to Memorize
The words of Baptism

Things to Do at Home

1. Ask your parents why they chose the name they gave you.
2. Find out more about the way your patron saint imitated Christ.
3. Prepare to explain in class how a baby is baptized.
4. Learn how the RCIA program is carried out in your parish.
5. Make a poster that tells what Baptism does for us.

We Remember

What is Baptism?
Baptism is the sacrament through which we die and rise with Christ. It cleanses us from sin, gives us a share in God's own life, and makes us members of the Christian community, the Church.

What are sacramentals?
Sacramentals are words, actions, and objects blessed by the Church that bring us closer to God.

We Respond

May almighty God, who has given us a new birth by water and the Holy Spirit, guard us from evil and keep us faithful to him.
Rite of Baptism

Sacramentals
Blessing of the priest, bishop, pope; ashes; candles; crucifixes; medals; Mary; scapulars; images; statues of the saints and Mary; Stations of the Cross; Holy card; church building

19

We Review

Sacrament Match   Write the letter of the word that matches the sentence best. Not all words will be used. Words may be used twice.

A. sacrament   **C.** catechumen   **E.** original sin   **G.** Eucharist
B. sacramental   **D.** Baptism   **F.** chrism   **H.** RCIA

_B_ **1.** Blessing pets on the feast of St. Francis of Assisi

_H_ **2.** Process for adults who wish to become Catholic

_E_ **3.** Sin we were born with that is taken away by Baptism

_H_ **4.** Rite that includes all three sacraments of initiation

_F_ **5.** Name of one holy oil used in Baptism

_C_ **6.** A person who is learning to become a Catholic

_B_ **7.** An object, such as a blessed medal, that helps us come closer to God

_D_ **8.** The first sacrament, which fills us with God's life

Signs of Life   Draw a line matching the symbol with what it stands for.

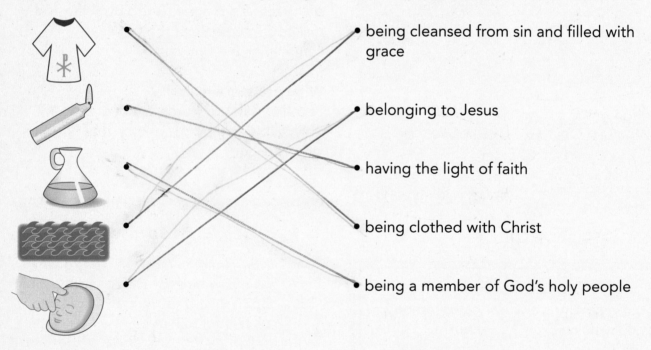

- being cleansed from sin and filled with grace
- belonging to Jesus
- having the light of faith
- being clothed with Christ
- being a member of God's holy people

The Words of the Rite   In an emergency anyone can baptize. Fill in the words that must be said as water is poured over the person's head.

I _____ you in the _____ of the Father, and of the

_____ , and of the Holy _____ .

confirmation
- *fullness of the Holy Spirit*
- *witness christ* — *recommit*
- *strong wind* *ourselves to*
- *tongues of* *our baptismal*
fire *promises*
- *Pentecost*
- *chism*

baptism
- *Holy Spirit*
- *witness to christ*
- *commit ourselves*
to baptismal
promises
- *forever belong*
to God
- *chism*

The Holy Spirit Strengthens the Church's Faith

According to the Acts of the Apostles, ten days after his Ascension, Jesus kept his promise to send the Holy Spirit upon the apostles. The Holy Spirit came to strengthen their faith and make them strong witnesses to Jesus.

On that day they were all together in the room where the Last Supper had taken place. Mary was with them. Suddenly the sound of a strong wind filled the house. A flame, like a tongue of fire, rested above the head of each person there. The flames were a sign that the Holy Spirit had come. The apostles felt the Spirit's strength renewing them.

With great courage the apostles went out and began to speak about Jesus. A large crowd gathered. Because it was the Jewish feast of Pentecost, there were many visitors in Jerusalem. Most of them spoke and understood only the language of their own country. Yet, when the apostles spoke, everyone could understand what they said!

Deeply changed by the faith of the apostles, people asked to be baptized. That day some three thousand people were welcomed into the Church.

As the days passed, the apostles spread the message of Jesus in many towns and villages. They baptized many people. When they laid their hands on them, believers received the Holy Spirit. The apostles were witnesses to Jesus everywhere they went. Their faith gave them the strength to suffer and die for Jesus and his kingdom.

The Spirit Comes in Confirmation

Today Christ continues to send the Holy Spirit. The Spirit strengthens our faith and unites us more closely to Jesus and the Church in the Sacrament of Confirmation. In Confirmation we recommit ourselves to living out our baptismal promises. In the Eastern Catholic Churches, Confirmation is called *chrismation*. It is celebrated at Baptism along with the Eucharist, as in the days of the early Church. In the RCIA, the priest confirms the catechumens.

Let's visit St. Mary Parish, where the bishop is coming for Confirmation this evening. Mr. Rini's fifth graders wonder what will take place during the ceremony. He explains the rite.

Carlos: Why does the bishop come for Confirmation?

Mr. R: The bishop usually confirms. He takes the place of the apostles in a special way. After Jesus sent the Holy Spirit, the apostles went out and gave the Holy Spirit to others. They were the first bishops of the Church.

Chris: My brother Cory is being confirmed. He's been meeting every week with our neighbor to prepare.

Mr. R: Your neighbor is Cory's sponsor. He's agreed to help your brother live as a Christian. During the ceremony the sponsor will stand with his right hand on Cory's shoulder while he's being confirmed.

Jan: Will there be a Mass tonight?

Mr. R: Yes. The Sacrament of Confirmation usually takes place during the Mass. After the bishop's homily, all those to be confirmed stand and renew their baptismal promises.

Monica: That's just what we did at our First Communion!

Mr. R: Right. Then the bishop asks the people to pray with him. He asks that God will pour out the Holy Spirit upon the confirmation candidates. The Spirit will strengthen their faith and enable them to become more like Christ. Sean, do you remember how the apostles gave the Holy Spirit to others?

Sean: Yes. The apostles laid their hands on those who were to receive the Holy Spirit.

Mr. R: Good. Tonight the bishop and any priests who may join him in confirming will extend their hands over those to be confirmed. They will pray for the gifts of the Spirit.

Anita: How is a person confirmed?

Mr. R: The bishop anoints the person with chrism on the forehead with the laying on of his hand and says, "Be sealed with the gift of the Holy Spirit."

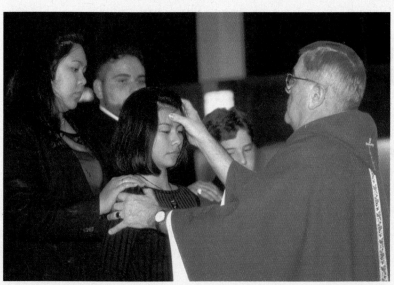

Tawana: What does it mean to be "sealed"?

Mr. R: It means that the person now belongs completely to God. He or she is marked forever as a witness to Christ. The Holy Spirit gives that person grace to witness to Christ in the world. Do you remember what witness means, Sandra?

Sandra: It means to show by words and actions that you are a follower of Christ.

Mr. R: That's it. Chrism is a sweet-smelling oil. Anthony, can you think of reasons why oil should be used?

Anthony: Well, some athletes use oil to rub their muscles after a workout. The oil soothes and gives strength. I guess chrism is a sign of the strength we receive in Confirmation. The sacrament helps us to live the Christian life.

Mr. R: Good! The Sign of the Cross the bishop makes in the anointing reminds us that we must be willing to profess our faith. We must be ready even to die for it.

Randy: Mr. Rini, the boys and girls who receive Confirmation tonight really have a lot to live up to, haven't they?

Mr. R: Yes, Randy. But let's remember the Holy Spirit is powerful. Recall what he did for the apostles and others. He continues to do wonderful things for his people in this sacrament. You can begin now to prepare for your Confirmation. You can pray to the Holy Spirit and live each day in a Christlike way.

Search

Fill in the missing words. You can find them on pages 22 and 23.

1. The usual minister of Confirmation is the _____.

2. A person called a _____ helps the candidate prepare for Confirmation.

3. The candidates renew their baptismal _____.

4. The holy oil used in Confirmation is called _____.

5. An important sign of the sacrament is the _____ on of hands.

6. The words used in Confirmation are "Be sealed with the _____ of the Holy Spirit."

7. I will get ready for Confirmation by praying to the _____ and by living

each day in a _____ way.

The Holy Spirit Makes Us Strong Witnesses

In Baptism you were called to be a witness to Jesus and to work for the Church. Confirmation is your chance to declare your faith and renew your baptismal promises for yourself. The Holy Spirit who comes to you in Confirmation strengthens you to follow your baptismal call. The Spirit will enable you to know Jesus better, love him more, and be more like him. The Spirit will make you a strong witness to Jesus.

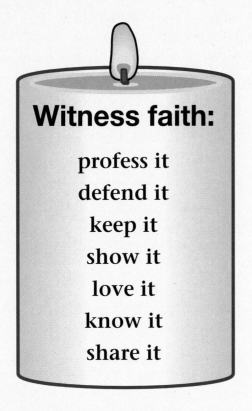

Witness faith:

profess it

defend it

keep it

show it

love it

know it

share it

To give witness to Jesus means to:

+ pray as Jesus prayed
+ love and serve God as Jesus did
+ love and serve others as Jesus did
+ follow the teachings of Jesus and his Church
+ spread the Good News to others
+ work for the Church

As a Christian it is your privilege and duty to give witness to Jesus. When you do, your

faith becomes like a light that shows other people how good Jesus is. Seeing your witness, they are led to believe in him and love him.

You can give witness by working for the Church, in any of several ways. Helping in parish activities is one way. Supporting the missions is another. The missions may be parishes in poor areas of our own country or in other countries where people are just beginning to learn about God. Priests, brothers, sisters, and laypersons who work in missions are called **missionaries**.

Missionaries need your help to spread the Good News and make the Church grow. You can help by offering your prayers and your gifts of food, clothing, or money. You may even become missionaries yourselves when you get older. Some young people volunteer to serve on missions at home or overseas for one year or more. They join the Maryknoll Lay Missioners, Jesuit Volunteers, or other groups. You do not need to wait for Confirmation to be witnesses. All baptized Christians are called to give witness to Jesus. In Confirmation the Holy Spirit will strengthen your faith and your love. You will be able to show you are a follower of Jesus even when it is hard.

5 Another way to witness is to support the Church by donating money, equipment, and supplies. It is Church law that members provide for the material needs of the Church as far as they are able. You might give part of your allowance to the Sunday collection.

Fill out the certificate below. Design the seal for it.

My Plan and Promise Certificate

Name _____Tarmily Wen_____ Date __Oct. 4, 2006__

I plan to be confirmed when I am ____12____ years old.

I have ____2.____ years to get ready.

I promise to get ready by doing the things I have checked below.

_____ Pray to the Holy Spirit daily

_____ Celebrate Sunday liturgies and receive Holy Communion

_____ Receive the Sacrament of Reconciliation regularly

__✓__ Do my share to help at home

__✓__ Show respect for other people

__✓__ Forgive those who have hurt me

_____ Read the Gospels and study my religion

_____ Share the goodness of Jesus with others

_____ Help the poor and the missions

SEAL OF PROMISE

Father Damien, "Martyr of Molokai"

Joseph de Veuster was born in Belgium on January 3, 1840. While at college he decided God was calling him to be a priest. He joined the same community his brother had joined and took the name Damien. His brother became very ill and was unable to go to his mission in Hawaii. Damien offered to go in his place. He arrived in Hawaii and was ordained in Honolulu.

For nine years Damien served the people in different villages. He was interested in a leper settlement on the island of Molokai. The colony was very poor, and there was not one doctor or priest on the island. Father Damien offered to go to Molokai and work with the lepers.

All the people who could still walk came to meet the boat to see the priest who wanted to work with them. They were sure he wouldn't stay very long when he saw what life there was like. Lepers often have unpleasant sores, and some even lose fingers and toes because of the disease. Some lepers who were not very ill lived a wild life, since there were no laws and no police on the island.

Father Damien got busy right away, cleaning up the huts, nursing the very sick people, and trying new medicines. Those able to help were put to work building decent houses. Father Damien not only preached and offered Mass, but he built roads, water systems, orphanages, and churches. He even started a choir and a band! He made the people feel they were important, so they began to take better care of themselves and their property. Damien also begged for money to help his six hundred lepers. Joseph Dutton, a layman from Vermont, joined him in his work.

On Sundays Father Damien always began his homily with "My dear lepers." One day he said, "My fellow lepers." At first it was very quiet. Then people began to sob. They knew that their beloved Father Damien had gotten the disease. Even when ill, he carried on his work. A group of Franciscan Sisters from New York, under the leadership of Mother Marianne, came to help.

Father Damien died when he was forty-nine years old. Can you explain why he can be called "Martyr of Molokai"? Do you know someone who is a witness like Father Damien today?

he was beatified by the Pope in 1995. Step to sainthood

Things to Do at Home

1. Find pictures of people giving witness to Christ. Find pictures of people *not* giving witness and tell how they could.
2. Learn the gifts of the Holy Spirit.
3. Ask the Holy Spirit how to give witness to Christ this evening.

We Remember

What is Confirmation?
Confirmation is a sacrament through which the Holy Spirit strengthens our faith professed in Baptism, unites us more closely to the Church, commits us to Christ, and helps us witness to him.

Words to Know

sponsor   witness

We Respond

Come, Holy Spirit. Strengthen my faith, increase my hope, deepen my love.

We Review

Ring the Right Words   Circle the answers to the questions.

1. Who helps someone prepare for Confirmation?

   (the sponsor)   the candidate

2. What is the oil used in Confirmation?

   chrismation   (chrism)

3. When did the Holy Spirit come with power to the apostles?

   Ascension   (Pentecost)

4. What promises do people renew in Confirmation?

   (baptismal)   eucharistic

5. What words are said during the anointing at Confirmation?

   "Be anointed."   ("Be sealed.")

A Witness   Name two ways to witness to Jesus:

I could be a witness by telling people what I learn in school.

I could be a witness by giving money to the mission

Jesus Feeds Us in the Eucharist

Why do you get hungry? Your body is telling you it needs food. Food keeps you strong, healthy, and full of energy. It helps you grow. God's life in you needs to grow and become strong too. To nourish this life Jesus gave us the Sacrament of the Holy Eucharist. This sacrament of initiation is the heart of Christian worship. It is the center of Christian life.

For the chosen people the central act of history was their deliverance by God from slavery in Egypt. Death passed over them. They remember this event every year by observing the feast of **Passover,** or *Pasch*, which includes a special meal. When Jesus celebrated the Passover meal the night before he died, he gave it a new meaning. During the Last Supper he offered himself to the Father for us. The next day, through his sacrifice on Calvary, he passed over from death to life. With him we pass over from death to life.

During the meal Jesus said, "Do this in memory of me." Whenever we celebrate the Eucharist, we remember Jesus' saving us through the **Paschal Mystery.** The Paschal Mystery is the passion, death, resurrection, and ascension of Jesus. We not only celebrate the Paschal Mystery at Mass but are invited to enter into it. Daily at Mass, Jesus

offers the Father the same sacrifice he offered on the cross. Daily he offers us the Bread of Life and the cup of salvation.

God fed his people in earlier times. When the Hebrews escaped from Egypt, God sent them quail and manna. Manna was a kind of bread, which kept them alive in the

desert. Jesus satisfied people's hunger too. To feed a crowd listening to him teach, he multiplied bread and fish.

When we receive Holy Communion, we receive the risen Jesus. Jesus is present at Mass in his Word, in his priest, and in his people. But during Mass he also becomes present in a special way through the words of the priest, "This is my body" and "This is my blood." We call Jesus' presence in the Blessed Sacrament the *real presence.* Under the forms of bread and wine, Jesus feeds us with himself. We become one with him, the Father, and the Holy Spirit. We are united with all his people who share the meal with us.

In the Eucharist, Jesus forgives our sins if we are sorry. His life in us grows, helping us to overcome temptations and to live according to his Word. Nourished by Jesus, we become like him. He fills us with his love so we can be more concerned about others. He gives us strength to forgive. He enables us to accept sufferings and to make sacrifices.

Jesus made his apostles priests at the Last Supper. He gave them, and all bishops and priests, the power to make the Paschal Mystery present. Baptized members of Jesus' family, the Church, join with the priest in the celebration. Millions of Catholics around the world celebrate the Eucharist. In each country members of Christ's Body bring to the celebration their own customs, but all are one in offering the same sacrifice.

Do you want to grow in God's love and grace? Accept his invitation to celebrate the Eucharist and receive him in Communion as often as you can. The Church wisely has made it a law that Catholics receive Communion at least once during the Easter season.

Mass is offered on an **altar,** which is a sign of Christ. Why is it fitting that an altar is used for the Eucharist? Write your reasons here.

It is fitting because represent a table

We Prepare to Receive Jesus

We prepare our hearts to receive Jesus. We desire to receive him, we try to be loving to others, and we try to keep free from sin. The Eucharist is a sign of union with God and the Church. Mortal sin separates a person from God and his people; therefore, it must be confessed in the Sacrament of Reconciliation before a person goes to Communion.

We prepare for Holy Communion by fasting. We do not eat or drink anything except water and medicine for one hour before Communion. The sick and aged and those who care for them need not fast.

We also prepare to receive Jesus in the first part of the Mass. During it we pray together, asking God to forgive our sins. Then we hear God's Word, which helps us receive Jesus with greater love and gratitude.

In the next unit you will learn about all the parts of the eucharistic celebration. Then you will be able to join in our greatest act of worship more fully.

Can You Identify These Vessels and Vestments?

Here are special vessels and vestments that are used at Mass. Write their names under them. Look for these objects the next time you celebrate the Eucharist.

ciborium–container that holds the hosts

paten–a plate that holds the hosts

chalice–cup containing the wine

cruets–small pitchers that hold the water and wine

purificator–white cloth used to dry the priest's fingers, the chalice, and the paten

corporal–square, white cloth unfolded and spread under the chalice, paten, and ciborium

pall–small, hard, linen square sometimes used to cover the chalice to protect the wine

alb–priest's long, white robe

chasuble–garment worn over the alb; its color changes with the seasons

stole–long, narrow scarf worn around the neck

1. _pall_   2. _stole_   3. _ciborium_

4. _alb_   5. _corporal_   6. _paten_   7. _chalice_

8. _purificator_   9. _chasuble_   10. _cruets_

**The hand of the Lord feeds us;
He answers all our needs.**

Let all your works give you thanks, O Lord,
and let your faithful ones bless you.
Let them discourse of the glory of your kingdom
and speak of your might.

**The hand of the Lord feeds us;
He answers all our needs.**

The eyes of all look hopefully to you,
and you give them their food in due season;
You open your hand
and satisfy the desire of every living thing.

**The hand of the Lord feeds us;
He answers all our needs.**

The Lord is just in all his ways
and holy in all his works.
The Lord is near to all who call upon him,
to all who call upon him in truth.

**The hand of the Lord feeds us;
He answers all our needs.**

Responsorial Psalm: Psalm 145
Mass of the Holy Eucharist

We Honor Christ's Presence in the Eucharist

After Communion the Blessed Sacrament is placed in the tabernacle. We honor the Lord present in the **tabernacle** by genuflecting. A sanctuary lamp burns near the tabernacle as long as Jesus is there. It too is a way to honor Jesus.

When we visit Jesus in the Blessed Sacrament and pray quietly, we come to know him better. He helps us to become true Christians who love and serve as he did.

A priest may take a sacred host from the tabernacle for someone who is sick or dying. Receiving Jesus in Holy Communion gives strength and comfort to the person. **Eucharistic ministers** too may take Holy Communion to the sick and others who are not able to come to church. These ministers who carry the Lord to members of the community are specially chosen. They must try to live like Christ and be a light to others.

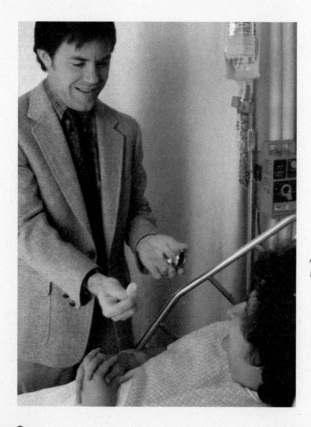

Sometimes the Holy Eucharist is made visible for us to adore. During **exposition** the Blessed Sacrament is put into a **monstrance.** This is a sacred vessel with a metal holder that lets us view the sacred host. It is placed on the altar. By prayer, song, readings, and processions we worship Christ the Lord.

Exposition ends with **Benediction.** The priest or deacon kneels at the altar. A song is sung while the Blessed Sacrament is incensed. The sweet-smelling incense is a sign of our prayers ascending to God. After a time of silent prayer, the priest or deacon says this or another prayer:

pyx

> Lord our God,
> You have given us the true bread
> from heaven.
> In the strength of this food may we
> live always
> by your life and rise in glory on the
> last day.
> We ask this through Christ our Lord.

Everyone answers, "Amen."

Then, with the monstrance, the priest or deacon makes the Sign of the Cross over us. He covers his hands with his vestment to show it is really Jesus who gives us this blessing. We make the Sign of the Cross as we are blessed. Sometimes we pray the Divine Praises. During the concluding song the Blessed Sacrament is put back into the tabernacle.

The Divine Praises

Blessed be God.
Blessed be his holy name.
Blessed be Jesus Christ, true God and true man.
Blessed be the name of Jesus.
Blessed be his most sacred heart.
Blessed be his most precious blood.
Blessed be Jesus in the most holy sacrament of the altar.
Blessed be the Holy Spirit, the Paraclete.

Blessed be the great mother of God, Mary most holy.
Blessed be her holy and immaculate conception.
Blessed be her glorious assumption.
Blessed be the name of Mary, virgin and mother.
Blessed be St. Joseph, her most chaste spouse.
Blessed be God in his angels and in his saints.

Viatican com

We Adore Jesus Present in Our Tabernacles

Prayer

Lord Jesus, I believe that you are present here in the Blessed Sacrament. I adore you, I believe in you, I hope in you, and I love you. You gave us the Eucharist to be with us and to strengthen us. Thank you for loving us so much.

O LORD, you know me well;
>   you know when I sit and when I stand;
>   you understand my thoughts from afar.
My journeys and my rest you watch over,
>   with all my ways you are familiar.
Even before a word is on my tongue,
>   behold, O LORD, you know the whole of it.
Behind me and before, you hem me in
>   and rest your hand upon me.
>   adapted from Psalm 139:1–5

Readings

Leader: One day Jesus fed many people who came to hear him speak. He felt sorry for the crowd because the people were hungry. In his love and goodness he fed thousands. The food that Jesus offers us today is his Body and Blood, his own life. Let's listen to what Jesus tells us about the living bread.

Reader 1:   I am the bread of life; whoever comes to me will never hunger, and whoever believes in me will never thirst. (John 6:35)

Reader 2:   The bread of God is that which comes down from heaven and gives life to the world. (John 6:33)

Reader 3:   Whoever eats my flesh and drinks my blood has eternal life, and I will raise him on the last day. For my flesh is true food, and my blood is true drink. (John 6:54–55)

Reader 4:   Whoever eats my flesh and drinks my blood remains in me and I in him. (John 6:56)

Leader: Let us think quietly for a few minutes about the words of Jesus and tell him how much we want him to be with us.

Song

Things to Do at Home

1. Write or find a prayer that you will use as your thanksgiving prayer after Holy Communion.
2. Make a visit to church if possible. Pray silently, thinking about how much Jesus loves you.
3. Think about how Jesus showed his love as you read one of these Scripture stories: Luke 10:38–42 or John 12:1–8.
4. Find out about St. Tarcisius, St. Clare, St. Gerard Majella, or St. Paschal Baylon. Write a report about the saint.

We Remember

Why is the Eucharist the greatest sacrament?
The Eucharist is the greatest sacrament because it is the risen Lord present with us. He offers the same sacrifice he offered on the cross. In Holy Communion he feeds us and unites us with himself and one another.

How do we prepare for Communion?
We prepare for Communion by desiring Jesus, by trying to be loving to others, by being free from mortal sin, and by fasting for one hour before Communion.

We Respond

O Sacrament most holy,
O Sacrament divine,
All praise and all thanksgiving
Be every moment thine.

We Review

Word Match Match the words with the descriptions.

A. Eucharist

B. Passover

C. Last Supper

D. Paschal Mystery

E. Benediction

F. exposition

_____ 1. the passion, death, resurrection, and ascension of Jesus

_____ 2. the central act of worship for Christians

_____ 3. when Jesus gave us the gift of the Eucharist

_____ 4. meal that celebrates God's deliverance of the Israelites

_____ 5. blessing of the people with the Blessed Sacrament

Word Scramble   Unscramble the mixed-up word in each sentence about the Eucharist. Complete the words in the box.

1. Jesus gives himself as our food to PLEH us think, speak, and act like him.
2. Receiving Holy Communion tells Jesus we want to be INTEUD with him and his people.
3. We prepare for Holy Communion by STINGAF for one hour before Communion.
4. With Jesus we have the GNESRTHT to overcome temptation.

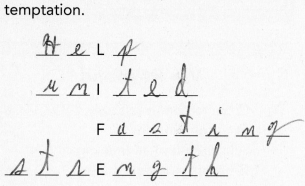

H e L p
u m i t e d
F a s t i n g
s t r e n g t h

Find the Reason   Find the reason in the second column that completes the statement in the first column. Place the correct letter on the line.

1. We need the Eucharist because ___B___.

2. One reason why the Blessed Sacrament is kept in the tabernacle at church is ___A___.

3. We make visits to church whenever we can because ___D___.

4. At the Eucharist we celebrate ___C___.

A. the sick and the dying might need Communion

B. we are weak and are tempted to be selfish

C. Jesus' saving us from sin and death

D. we want to adore the Lord present in the Blessed Sacrament

On Trial for Being Christian

Setting: The jury (class) is seated. The defendant, attorney, and witnesses are in their places. The judge is outside the room.

Officer: Court is now in session to hear the case of the People vs. B. Christian. Judge _____ is presiding. All rise.

(Judge enters and is seated. All sit.)

Judge: *(Pounding gavel)* This court will now come to order. What charges do you bring against the defendant, B. Christian?

Attorney: Your Honor, the defendant, B. Christian, has been accused of being a follower of Jesus. He has been accused of praying three times a day, of sharing with those in need, and of repeated acts of kindness and forgiveness.

Judge: B. Christian, do you understand the charges brought against you?

B. Christian: Yes, your Honor!

Judge: Call your first witness.

Attorney: Will Mr. C. Everything please come forward?

(C. Everything comes to the stand.)

Officer: Place your right hand on the Bible. Do you swear that what you say here today will be the whole truth and nothing but the truth, so help you God?

C. Everything: I do!

Attorney: Will you please tell the court what you saw the defendant, B. Christian, doing on the day of Thursday, September 8?

C. Everything: Yes, I most certainly will. On that day B. Christian left his house early in the morning. I was curious, so I followed him. He went to church and prayed and joined in the singing at Mass. I also know that B. Christian praises and thanks God before and after he eats. Besides that he has been seen praying before he goes to bed at night.

Attorney: Thank you.

(C. Everything returns to his place.)

Judge: Please call your next witness.

Attorney: Will Mrs. Need-a-Hand please come forward and take the stand?

(Mrs. Need-a-Hand comes and sits.)

Officer: Mrs. Need-a-Hand, place your right hand on the Bible. Do you swear that what you say here today will be the whole truth and nothing but the truth, so help you God?

Mrs. Need-a-Hand: I do!

Attorney: Would you please tell this court what happened to you on the afternoon of October 18?

Mrs. Need-a-Hand: Yes, I most certainly will. Because I am older, it is very difficult for me to get around. That day in October my yard was covered with fallen leaves. B. Christian came and raked them for me. Mind you, he didn't even want any money for it. He also went to the store for me. He wouldn't let me pay him for that either. And do you know how he did those things? He did them very cheerfully. I had been pretty crabby that day, but I was not able to stay crabby when B. Christian was around.

Attorney: Thank you, Mrs. Need-a-Hand. You may step down. Your Honor, I would like to call A. Classmate to the stand.

(A. Classmate comes forward.)

Officer: Place your right hand on the Bible. Do you swear that what you say will be the whole truth and nothing but the truth, so help you God?

A. Classmate: I do!

Attorney: Will you please tell the court how B. Christian has affected your life?

A. Classmate: Many boys and girls often made fun of me. I did not enjoy coming to school until one day B. Christian asked me whether I would sit next to him at lunch. We became good friends. Not only that, but one day he let me use his brand-new bike. He also told the other boys and girls how good I am at imitating animals. Now many people ask me to share my talent with them.

Attorney: Thank you, A. Classmate. You may step down.

Judge: You have now heard the evidence. We ask the jury to come to a decision about the defendant. We ask everyone who is not a member of the jury to wait quietly outside the room while the jury discusses the case.

(When the jury has reached a verdict, the officer calls the others back into the room.)

Jury Head: Your Honor, we have come to a decision.

Judge: How do you find the defendant?

Jury Head: We find the defendant _____.

Judge: *(Only if the verdict is "guilty")*: B. Christian, the jury has carefully weighed all the evidence and has found you guilty of being a Christian. Because they have found you guilty, I, by the power granted to me by this court, sentence you to _____ . *(Judge pounds gavel.)* Case closed!

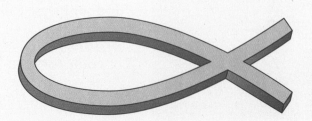

Prayer

Help me, Jesus, to spread your light everywhere I go. Fill my soul completely with your spirit and life. Then let your light shine through me so that every person I meet will feel your presence in my soul. Let others look and see no longer me but only you.

Stay with me, Jesus, and I will be your light to others. The light I give to others will be coming from you; none of it will be mine. Let me praise you in the way you love best—by letting others know you, not so much by my words, but by my joyful spirit and example. It will be you shining on others through me.

Amen.

Adapted from
Cardinal Newman's prayer
"Radiating Christ"

Sacrament Banner

Use the clues at the bottom and the words around the banner to fill in the sacrament acrostic.

Baptism anointing monstrance

chrism Christ Pentecost

hand fast bishop catechumen

b i S h o p
h A n d
C a t e c h u m e n
c h R i s m
f A s t
M o n s t r a n c e
P E n t e c o s t
a N o i n t i n g
B a p T i s m
C h r i S t

S the usual minister of Confirmation

A what the bishop places over those to be confirmed as he anoints them

C a nonbaptized person in the RCIA who desires to become a Catholic

R the holy oil used in Confirmation

A what we do for one hour before Holy Communion

M sacred vessel used to expose the Blessed Sacrament

E the day when Jesus gave the Holy Spirit to the apostles

N the rubbing with oil that means a person is strengthened to live the faith

T the sacrament in which we receive our first call to witness to Jesus

S the person the Holy Spirit helps us imitate

40

Puzzle in Review

How well do you remember what you've studied so far about Christian worship? Use the words below if you need help for any answers.

Confirmation   worship   Benediction   bread
Baptism   water   grace   faith
Eucharist   sacramentals   liturgy   RCIA
sacraments

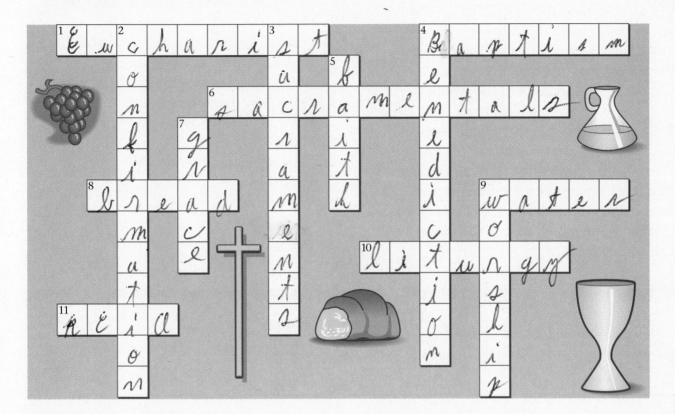

Across

1. Nourishes our life in Christ

4. The sacrament that makes us children of God and members of the Church

6. Words, actions, or objects blessed by the Church to bring us closer to God

8. One of the signs used in the Sacrament of the Eucharist

9. The chief sign used in the Sacrament of Baptism

10. The public worship of the Church

11. The process for initiating adults into the Church

Down

2. The sacrament in which we receive the Holy Spirit and recommit ourselves to witness to Jesus

3. Sacred signs in which we meet Jesus and receive grace

4. A blessing given by making the Sign of the Cross with the Blessed Sacrament

5. Belief in God increased through the sacraments

7. The gift of sharing in the life of God

9. Prayer and good deeds done to honor God

Looking Back at Unit 1

In this unit you have seen that Jesus comes to us through the Holy Spirit. He helps us give perfect worship to the Father. With Jesus we can rise above the power of sin. We can love and honor God as we should. You have learned about the sacraments of initiation—Baptism, Confirmation, and the Eucharist. They enable us to work with Christ for the salvation of the whole world.

In Baptism we begin to be Christians. Every day we are called to live the Christian life. We are strengthened to grow in this life through Confirmation. In the Eucharist, Jesus offers himself for us and nourishes us. United with him, we are able to share his love with others.

Living the Message

Can you give yourself a check (√) for each statement?

☑ I use sacramentals to help me remember that God loves me and has made me his child.

☑ I take time each day to praise and thank God for all he has done for me.

❏ Whenever I receive the Eucharist, I tell Jesus how much I love him.

☑ I give witness to Jesus by my good words and kind acts.

☑ I ask Jesus to help me when I am tempted.

Planning to Grow

Draw a picture of something you will do each day to worship God.

Ojo de Dios: The Eye of God

In the Loza family's home each bedroom has an ojo de Dios on the wall. This is a popular decoration that has its origins with the Huichol Indians in Mexico and the Pueblo tribe in the United States. To the Indians, the ojo de Dios was a good luck piece that could ward off evil. *Ojo de Dios* means "eye of God." The diamond pattern in the middle of the design stands for the eye of God, while the bands of color around it stand for God's wisdom and light flowing out to us.

Christians can easily adopt the ojo de Dios as a reminder of God's presence and providence, especially since it is made on two sticks in the form of a cross. Your family might make one to display in your house. You might also give one to relatives and friends as a sign of your wishes for God's blessings on them.

How to Make an Ojo de Dios

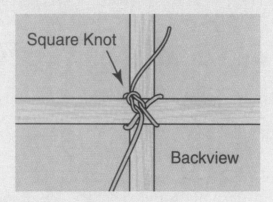

1. Cross two sticks. These can be dowels or ice cream sticks. Glue or tie the sticks together where they cross. (For a more professional piece, cut a small piece out of one of the sticks and set the other in it.) Tie yarn to sticks using square knots. Leave a short tail so you can tie the other end of the yarn to it when you are done.

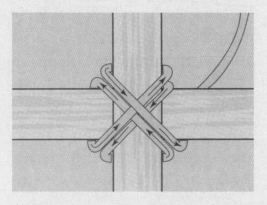

2. Wrap the yarn around one stick and then over and under the next stick. Continue this winding pattern, holding the yarn tight as you wind it.

3. Keep winding the yarn around the sticks. Lay each piece of yarn down next to the yarn before it, keeping it in neat rows.

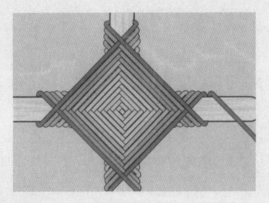

4. Change to yarn of another color by tying the new yarn to the end of the last color. Make sure the ends are behind a stick. Keep winding the yarn and make patterns with the colors.

Sacraments

In the puzzle find and circle the words listed here. Then write two sentences using as many of the words as you can.

worship	liturgy	altar
sacrifice	RCIA	Confirmation
Eucharist	oil	Communion
sacraments	Baptism	Benediction
grace	chrism	anointing
rite	sacramentals	faith

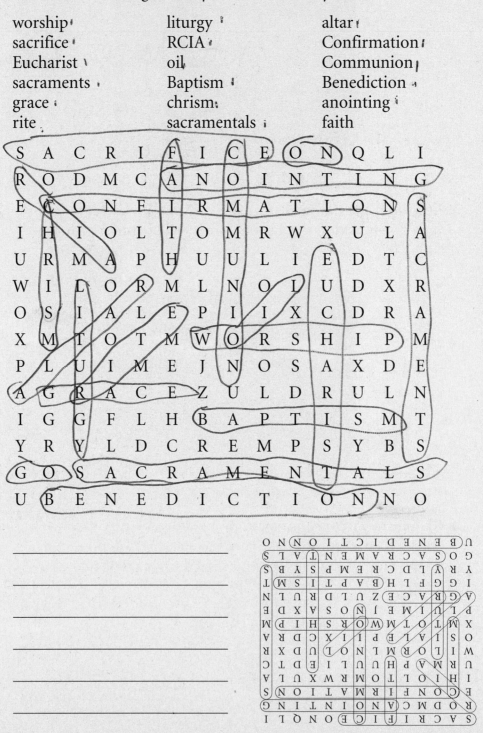

```
S A C R I F I C E O N Q L I
R O D M C A N O I N T I N G
E C O N F I R M A T I O N S
I H I O L T O M R W X U L A
U R M A P H U U L I E D T C
W I L O R M L N O L U D X R
O S I A L E P I I X C D R A
X M T O T M W O R S H I P M
P L U I M E J N O S A X D E
A G R A C E Z U L D R U L N
I G G F L H B A P T I S M T
Y R Y L D C R E M P S Y B S
G O S A C R A M E N T A L S
U B E N E D I C T I O N N O
```

_____

_____

_____

_____

_____

We Celebrate the Eucharist in Memory of Jesus

7

The Eucharist Is a Thanksgiving Celebration

We love celebrations! They help us to remember important events. They bring a group of people together. We do special things to celebrate the events.

The Eucharist is a celebration. For almost two thousand years Catholics have been gathering on the Lord's Day to celebrate Mass. We celebrate the Paschal Mystery of Jesus that saved us from sin and death and obtained eternal life for us. Through bishops and priests, the living Christ becomes present as bread and wine and offers himself to the Father in every Mass. The word *eucharist* means "thanksgiving." At the Eucharist we worship God and give him thanks. We already participate in the worship given God in heaven.

The special actions of the Mass show our faith and love as a community. Together we

ask God to free us from death and from sin, which separate us from him and one another. We ask for all we need in order to grow closer to God and to his people. We praise and thank him for his great goodness. We offer ourselves with Jesus to the Father for the coming of God's kingdom. We unite ourselves with Jesus, with the Father and the Holy Spirit, and with one another in Holy Communion, a special banquet. Then we go forth from the celebration to serve God and one another.

The third commandment is "Remember to keep holy the sabbath day." Church law tells us to do this by celebrating the Eucharist every Sunday. Why do you think God gave us the third commandment?

God gave me it so be part of the Eucharist and celebrate Paschal Mystery

A Yearlong Celebration

Our eucharistic celebrations have different themes. Throughout each **Church year,** the story of the mystery of Christ unfolds. We celebrate the coming of Jesus in Advent and Christmas. Then we celebrate his death and resurrection in Lent and Easter. These periods of time are called **seasons** of the Church year. Between the two major celebrations are weeks known as **Ordinary Time.** During the year we also celebrate special feasts such as the Ascension and Pentecost. In addition, certain days are feast days of Mary and other saints. Special prayers in the Mass honor the saints on their feast days and unite us to the liturgy of heaven.

Some Masses are for a special purpose. For instance, there are Masses for weddings and funerals, and there are Masses for needs like religious vocations and peace and justice. There are Masses to honor the Trinity and the Sacred Heart, and there are Masses for the dead.

The readings of the Mass, the prayers, the songs, and the color of the priest's vestments change according to the theme of the Mass.

What season of the Church year is it now?

Ordinary Time

If you were born on a feast day, what is it?

_____

What is your patron saint's feast day?

_____

The Supplement in the back of this book tells about some seasons and feast days.

The Church Year

Pentecost

All Saints Day

Ascension of the Lord

Advent

Immaculate Conception

Ordinary Time

Easter

Christmas

Easter Sunday / Ash Wednesday

Ordinary Time

A Community of Faith and Love

Baptism made us members of the new people of God, a community of faith and love. We celebrate together every week. We help one another grow in faith and love every day.

Name three people besides your parents who have helped your faith to grow.

My friend Nick, Luck, and Matt

Name three people besides your parents who have helped you to become a more loving and caring member of the Christian community. _Not Christian_

Write something you will do to help others grow in faith.

I will care for them

Write something you will do to help others grow in love.

I will share things with others.

The Rites of the Eucharist

All the prayers for Mass are found in a book called the **Sacramentary.** The Sacramentary is usually on the altar during the celebration. In this unit you will become more familiar with the rites of the Eucharist. Father Bob will explain the prayers and actions of the parts of the Mass.

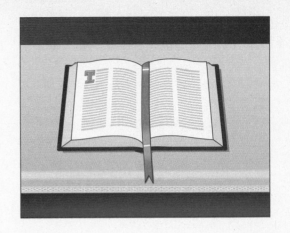

Introductory Rites
Entrance Procession and Song
Sign of the Cross and Greeting
Penitential Rite
Glory to God
Opening Prayer

Liturgy of the Word
First Reading
Responsorial Psalm
Second Reading
Alleluia or Gospel Acclamation
Gospel
Homily
Profession of Faith
General Intercessions

Liturgy of the Eucharist
Preparation of the Gifts
    Prayer over the Gifts
Eucharistic Prayer
    Preface
    Holy, Holy, Holy
    Institution Narrative and
        Consecration
    Offering
    Great Amen
Communion Rite
    Lord's Prayer
    Sign of Peace
    Breaking of the Bread:
        Lamb of God
    Communion
    Prayer after Communion

Concluding Rite
    Blessing
    Dismissal

The Introductory Rites Prepare Us for Worship

Prepare the way of the Lord.
Matthew 3:3

> **Introductory Rites**
> Liturgy of the Word
> Liturgy of the Eucharist
> Concluding Rite

The Mass is the most important prayer for us Catholics. We need to get ourselves ready for it. When we come to church, we may feel happy or sad. We may come with our friends or family, or we may come alone. We may be tired from rushing about or excited about what is going to happen that day.

To prepare ourselves for the eucharistic sacrifice, we remember why we have come. We have come to

✤ praise and thank God, who is so great and good;
✤ pray and sing of God's great love with the Christian community;
✤ hear God's Word and respond to it with love;
✤ offer ourselves as a gift with Jesus to God our Father;
✤ receive Jesus in Holy Communion and grow in his love.

When we arrive at church, we take holy water and bless ourselves. As we come into the presence of Christ, we genuflect, greet him, and adore him.

The Introductory Rites of the Mass are the prayers and actions at the beginning of the Mass. They prepare us to hear the Word of God, to offer ourselves with Jesus, and to receive him in Holy Communion. Father Bob will tell you about them.

Entrance Procession and Song

Members of the community who will have a special role in the Mass join me in a procession to the altar. Everyone praises God in joyful song or prayer. As a people who belong to God and who are on a journey to him, we come to worship God with faith and love.

Sign of the Cross and Greeting

We begin the Mass by making the Sign of the Cross. This sign reminds us that God loved us so much that he sent his Son to die for us. It reminds us that at our Baptism we were called to worship God our Father with Jesus.

I greet the community, recalling that God is present. Then I pray that God's grace and peace will be with everyone.

Penitential Rite

Through our sins and lack of love, we separate ourselves from God and his people. In the Penitential Rite we call upon the Lord to forgive our sins and to heal us.

When we pray, "Lord, have mercy," we show our trust in God's great mercy. We trust that God forgives us and gives us strength to live as his people.

Glory to God

This prayer is a powerful hymn praising almighty God. We pray it on most Sundays and on special feast days. The Glory to God is meant to be sung. If it is recited, it should still resound with life and joy. We should pray it with our whole hearts, for it speaks of the greatness of the all-holy God.

Opening Prayer

Now I invite everyone to pray by saying, "Let us pray." In silence we pray for our personal intentions and for those of the Church. Then I pray a prayer that asks for a special grace for all of us. By responding, "Amen," you say yes to this prayer. We are now ready to hear God speak his holy Word.

or so be it

Things to Do at Home

1. What is the last celebration you had at home? Write a paragraph explaining why it was a celebration. Then write a paragraph telling why we call Mass a celebration.
2. We dress in special ways for celebrations. Discuss with your parents how you can dress in a special way for next Sunday's eucharistic celebration.
3. Write a prayer asking Jesus to help you prepare to offer the eucharistic sacrifice with him. Ask him to help you love him and all his people more.
4. Ask a priest, an older person, and a young person why they go to Mass. Report back to your class.

We Remember

Why do we have Introductory Rites at Mass?
The Introductory Rites remind us that Jesus calls us together as a community of faith and love to worship the Father. They prepare us to listen to God's Word and to celebrate the Eucharist.

We Respond

Lord, help me to prepare for the eucharistic celebration by being a more loving member of the Christian community.

We Review

Five Facts   Answer these questions about the Eucharist.

What do we celebrate? _Paschal Mystery of Jesus_

When do we celebrate? _Mass_

What becomes the Body and Blood of Christ? _bread and wine_

What does the word *eucharist* mean? _Thansgiving_

What do we offer the Father besides Jesus? _We offer ourselves_

Word Scramble Unscramble the words.

1. A season of the Church year (TEERSA) _Easter_

2. Saint who has Masses in her honor (RMYA) _Mary_

3. Feast day celebrated by a special Mass (INSAONCSE) _Ascension_

4. Word that means yes (NEAM) _Amen_

5. What we ask the Lord for in the Penitential Rite (REYMC) _mercy_

6. Book containing prayers for Mass (AARMYCASETNR) _Sacramentary_

Name the Right Rite Here are the Introductory Rites of the Mass. List them in the correct order. After each one write the number of the phrase that best describes it.

Glory to God _Penitential Rite_ _5_

Opening Prayer _Opening Prayer_ _2_

Entrance Procession _Entrance Procession_ _3_

Penitential Rite _Sign of the Cross_ _1_

Sign of the Cross _Glory to God_ _4_

1. Our prayer asking for healing and forgiveness
2. The Church's prayer for a special grace
3. Action reminding us that we are a people on the way to our Father
4. Sign that we are saved by Jesus
5. A joyful prayer of praise

Introductory Rites
Liturgy of the Word
Liturgy of the Eucharist
Concluding Rite

God's Word Has a Message for Us

We welcome a letter from a friend. It reminds us that our friend loves us and is thinking of us. It may even tell us a secret that only we can know. We like to read it over and over again. We want to respond to our friend's message with love.

The Bible is the written Word of God. In the Mass, we receive a special message from God when we listen to the readings from the Bible. God speaks to us in Scripture. He warns us about what is evil and promises us eternal happiness if we hear his Word and keep it. God reminds us that he loves us more than anyone else does and invites us to love him in return. God gives us the power to follow his Word. We keep God's Word when we do whatever God tells us.

Jesus is called the Word of God. He brought the Father's message to life in all he said and did. He always did his Father's will. All that he did and said reminded the people of the Father's love and showed them how to live. Through his death and resurrection, Jesus brought new life. He told us that God has wonderful things prepared for those who hear his Word and keep it. When we hear and keep God's Word, it becomes alive and active in us.

In order to **listen** to God's Word, we pay close attention and think of God's loving presence. We listen with faith, believing what we hear with all our minds and hearts. We are still and try to let nothing disturb us. We let God speak to our hearts.

We should **respond** to God's Word every time we hear it. We think about it and pray about it. We can pray a psalm or we can pray in our own words. We can ask God to help us understand his Word and keep it with love.

Read each of the following stories and the readings. The readings are words of Jesus that could help the boy or girl in the story decide what to do. Discuss with your classmates what decision should be made and how the Scripture reading would help to make that decision.

✤ Jim and Matt were good friends, but they had a disagreement over a play in a soccer game. Jim thought that the play was out of bounds. Matt disagreed. They argued and soon got into a fight. Jim got a black eye. The next day Matt went to Jim's house and said, "I'm sorry."

Reading: Luke 17:4

I should forgive others

✤ Tony had been ill and out of school for several weeks. He had missed so much that he couldn't answer the teacher's questions or do the assignments. Everything was so hard that he was afraid he would never catch up.

Reading: Mark 4:37–41

Tony will catch up with God's help

✤ Debbie, a teenager, wanted to be popular. She went to a party with her friends. Some in the group were using drugs and encouraged her to join them. Debbie wanted to be part of the group, but she also wanted to be a follower of Jesus.

Reading: Mark 8:34–36

Don't risk being popular just follow Jesus

God Speaks through the Readings at Mass

After the Introductory Rites comes the first main part of the Mass, the **Liturgy of the Word.** During this time we listen with open minds and loving hearts as God speaks to us and teaches us. Father Bob will explain what happens. The readings for the day are found in a book called the **Lectionary.** This word comes from a Latin word that means "reading."

First Reading

The First Reading of a Sunday liturgy is usually taken from the Old Testament. Through these writings, God reveals his love and faithfulness in dealing with his people. We know in faith that God shows the same loving care for us today.

Responsorial Psalm

After listening to God's Word, we respond by praying a psalm. The psalms, song-prayers from the Hebrew Scriptures, were prayed by Jesus. We now join our prayers to his to praise the Father. Some psalms praise and thank God. Others express sorrow for sin or ask God's help.

Second Reading

The Second Reading at a Sunday Mass is usually taken from a letter of St. Paul or another apostle. These letters, called **epistles,** were written to early Christian communities to encourage the people to follow Jesus more closely. They instruct us and tell us to put aside our sins and follow Jesus.

After each of the two readings, the reader announces, "The Word of the Lord." Grateful for God's Word, we respond, "Thanks be to God."

Alleluia

The Alleluia, which brings a burst of new life to the Mass, is a special welcome to Christ, who will speak to us in the Gospel. We stand at attention, ready to do whatever he will tell us. We sing a joyful "alleluia" before and after a verse that is from the Bible. In Lent the Alleluia is replaced by another response of praise such as "Praise to you, Lord Jesus Christ, King of endless glory!"

The second Reading comes from the New Testament

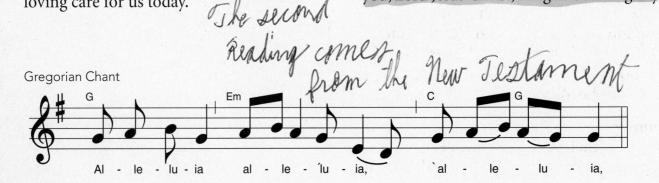

Gregorian Chant

Al - le - lu - ia al - le - ĺu - ia, `al - le - lu - ia,

Gospel

The Gospel tells of Jesus' life, death, and resurrection. It is Good News because it speaks of God's love and fills us with the hope of eternal happiness with God.

Jesus taught the people of his time about the Father's goodness and love. He taught them how to live as true children of his Father. He taught in the synagogue, on the hillside, from a boat, and in homes. He teaches the same lessons to us today every time the Gospel is read.

The deacon or I announce the Gospel by saying, "A reading from the Gospel according to _____," naming the Gospel. You proclaim, "Glory to you, Lord." We make the Sign of the Cross, touching our thumbs to our foreheads, our lips, and our hearts. We invite Christ to place his living Word in our minds, on our lips, and in our hearts. We are ready to welcome his Word.

At the end of the Gospel, the reader proclaims, "The Gospel of the Lord." You respond, "Praise to you, Lord Jesus Christ." You praise Christ himself, who is truly present in his Word.

Homily

After the readings at Mass, the deacon or I give a talk called a **homily.** We speak to you

sermon

in the name of Jesus. We try to help you understand God's message and encourage you to live it.

Profession of Faith

After the readings and homily we stand to respond in prayer. On Sundays and special feasts we pray the **Creed** together. In the Creed we tell God that we believe all that Jesus teaches us through the Church. We proclaim the truths of the faith we share as Catholic Christians. We begin by saying, "We believe in one God . . ."

General Intercessions

As people who believe in the loving care of our Father, we now respond to his Word by asking him to provide for our needs. Through the Prayer of the Faithful, we pray for the needs of all people. We pray for the Church, the Holy Father, and our bishop. We pray for the needs of the world, our own country, and our diocese and parish. We pray for people suffering from injustice and pain and for those who have died. We pray for people we know and love.

Write three petitions you would like to pray for during Mass:

Let us Pray for

The poor people here

The pets in the world

The weak babies in the world

Things to Do at Home

1. Print the Psalm response or the Gospel verse for Sunday on a card and post it where your family can refer to it.
2. In your family meal prayer, include a verse from the Sunday reading that gives a message to remember.
3. Discuss a thought from the Gospel or homily that will be an inspiration for the coming week.
4. You might memorize the Creed if you do not already know it by heart.

We Remember

What is the first main part of the Mass?
The first main part of the Mass is the Liturgy of the Word.

What happens during the Liturgy of the Word?
In the Liturgy of the Word, God speaks to us and teaches us.

Words to Know

Liturgy of the Word
Lectionary
epistle
homily
Creed

We Respond

Jesus be in my mind.
Jesus be on my lips.
Jesus be in my heart.

We Review

Responses What are the responses to the following statements? Write them.
The Word of the Lord.

Thanks to to be God

A reading from the Gospel according to Mark.

Glory to you, Lord

The Gospel of the Lord.

Praise to you Lord Jesus Christ

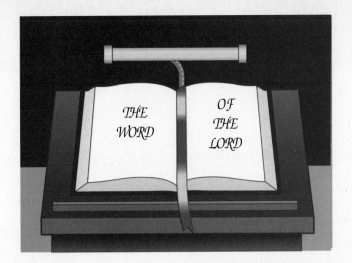

THE WORD OF THE LORD

Riddles Can you name me?

1. You pray me after hearing the First Reading at Mass. I am a song-prayer from the Old Testament.

psalm

2. I am the most important reading at Mass. I tell you about the life, death, and resurrection of Jesus.

Gospel

3. When you recite me, you tell everyone that you believe in Jesus and all he teaches through the Catholic Church.

Creed

4. I am the word of joyful praise that announces the Gospel.

Alleluia Glory to you, Lord

5. I am the prayers you say to ask our loving Father for blessings for all the people of the world.

General Intercessions

6. I am the part of the Mass in which the priest or deacon helps you understand God's message in the readings.

Homily

Missing Words Fill in the blanks to make true statements.

When the Bible is read at the Eucharist, ___*Jesus God*___ speaks to us.

Keeping God's Word means doing ___*whatever God tells us*___

The readings for the Mass are found in a book called the ___*Lectionary*___.

Introductory Rites
Liturgy of the Word
Liturgy of the Eucharist
Concluding Rite

We Thank God for His Great Goodness

When someone gives us a wonderful gift, we are grateful. In what ways can we show our gratitude?

I say thank you God. I give something in return I keep gift I don't like

We owe our greatest thanks to God, who has given us all these wonderful gifts:

✥ life
✥ family and good friends
✥ lovely flowers, crisp apples, and singing birds
✥ freedom to choose the good
✥ his own Son, Jesus, who freed us from sin and death and who teaches us how to live as children of God.

List three gifts from God for which you are especially grateful.

Thank you, God, for—

*My family
friends
life*

How can we show God that we are grateful for all his gifts? We would like to thank God by giving him a perfect gift. We can do this in the Eucharist. Do you recall what the word *eucharist* means? *thanksgiving*
redemption - redem

Jesus Is the Perfect Gift

At the Last Supper, Jesus gave thanks to the Father and offered himself as the perfect gift. He offered himself on the cross to save us from sin and prepare the way to eternal life. As a man, Jesus took our place and redeemed us. Because he is the Son of God, the gift he offered God our Father was perfect. God our Father accepted the gift of his Son Jesus. At the Last Supper, Jesus gave us a way to join him in offering his gift: the Eucharist. *Consecration*

The night before he died, Jesus took bread and a cup of wine. He said to his apostles, "Take and eat, this is my Body. Take and drink, this is the cup of my Blood." He then told them, "Do this in memory of me." With these words Jesus gave the apostles the power to do what he had just done. He gave us the Mass. *; priest*

Whenever we celebrate Mass, we unite ourselves with Jesus' sacrifice. We offer this perfect gift to the Father.

The Eucharist is our greatest prayer. We come into God's presence and remember God's saving acts and all his gifts. We share a meal as God's holy people. The Mass gives perfect praise and thanksgiving to God. It makes up for our sins and enables us to follow Jesus to eternal life.

How can I repay the LORD
for all the good done for me?
I will raise the cup of salvation
and call on the name of the LORD.

I will offer sacrifice of thanksgiving
and call on the name of the LORD.
I will pay my vows to the LORD
in the presence of all his people,
In the courts of the house of the LORD,
in your midst, O Jerusalem.
Psalm 116:12–13, 17–19

Jesus Is the Perfect Gift

We Offer Jesus' Sacrifice of Thanksgiving

In the Introductory Rites of the Mass, we speak to God. In the Liturgy of the Word, God speaks to us. In the Liturgy of the Eucharist, a gift is given to God, and then God gives a gift to us. Jesus offers himself with us to the Father and then gives himself to us in Holy Communion.

The Liturgy of the Eucharist includes the Preparation of the Gifts, the Eucharistic Prayer, and Communion. Again Father Bob will explain what happens.

Preparation of the Gifts

Members of the community present gifts of bread and wine to me. Bread and wine are basic food for people all over the world. They stand for us. They are signs of life and work as well as of unity. Bread is made from many grains of wheat, and wine is made from the juice of many grapes. At the Last Supper, Jesus prayed for the unity symbolized by the bread and wine. He prayed that we would all be one and would love one another. Money for the poor and for the Church may also be offered as signs of our life and work. They show that we want to care for one another. As these gifts are brought to the altar, we prepare to offer our hearts with Jesus.

You might offer to bring the bread and wine to the altar sometime. Remember that these gifts are a sign that you will be offering yourself, your joys, your sufferings, your good times, and your work.

I place the gifts of bread and wine on the altar. We praise God for giving us the bread. You may pray, "Blessed be God forever." Then I pour a little water into the wine. The water stands for us. Just as the water is joined to the wine that will become Jesus, so we will be joined to him. Then we praise God for the wine. You again may pray, "Blessed be God forever."

I wash my hands, asking God to cleanse me from my sin. Then I invite you to pray that God will accept our gifts. You pray,

> May the Lord accept the sacrifice at your hands
> for the praise and glory of his name,
> for our good, and the good of all his Church.

Then I say or sing a prayer over the gifts. You join my prayer by saying, "Amen."

Eucharistic Prayer

Now begins the most important prayer of the Mass: the Eucharistic Prayer. I invite you to praise and thank God. I sing or say, "Lift up your hearts." You answer, "We lift them up to the Lord." I say, "Let us give thanks to the Lord our God." You respond, "It is right to give him thanks and praise."

Preface and Holy, Holy, Holy

I then pray the Preface, a prayer of praise and thanksgiving, in your name. At the end of the Preface, we join our voices and sing, "Holy, holy, holy Lord," and cry out, "Hosanna," in praise of Jesus, who came from heaven to save us.

Institution Narrative and Consecration
Then I ask God to bless our gifts of bread and wine. I say the words Jesus said at the Last Supper. God **consecrates** the bread and wine: they become the Body and Blood of Jesus. When I show the bread and then the cup, there is a moment of silence. In our hearts we can say the prayer Thomas said when he saw Jesus after the resurrection: "My Lord and my God!" We can thank God for the great gift of his Son and for his saving deeds. Then I invite you to proclaim the mystery of our faith with me. We sing this or another **memorial acclamation:**

> When we eat this bread and drink this cup, we proclaim your death, Lord Jesus, until you come in glory.

Offering
As I continue the Eucharistic Prayer, the whole Church unites with Jesus in offering the gift of himself to the Father through the Holy Spirit. We offer ourselves with Jesus. We tell God that we are ready to do whatever he asks. Together with the whole Church, we pray for all the living and the dead. We ask to share eternal life with Mary and all the saints.

There are four main Eucharistic Prayers that we may choose to pray as well as several others. Listen carefully during this part of the Mass and see whether you can tell them apart.

Great Amen
The Eucharistic Prayer ends with a powerful acclamation. I lift up the cup and the host. I sing or say, "Through him, with him, in him, in the unity of the Holy Spirit, all glory and honor is yours, almighty Father, for ever and ever." Then you give an important response. You sing or say, "Amen," which means "It is true." You should proclaim it with joy and enthusiasm. It tells of your faith, your thanksgiving, and your praise. St. Jerome said that this "great amen" echoed like thunder through Rome in his time. In the Great Amen you proclaim a strong yes to the sacred prayers and actions of the Eucharistic Prayer and a commitment to whatever the Father asks of you.

Father Kolbe, like Jesus, Offered Himself

During the Second World War, Father Maximilian Kolbe gave shelter to thousands of Polish people, both Christians and Jews. He risked his life to help these suffering people. On February 17, 1941, he was caught and sent to prison in Warsaw. A guard who saw his Franciscan habit and his rosary asked, "Do you believe in Christ?" Father Kolbe answered, "Yes, I do." Then the guard struck him in the face. Father Kolbe kept giving the same answer, and the guard kept beating him.

After that, Father Kolbe was given a striped convict's uniform and the number 16670. He was sent to a concentration camp, where he endured very hard work and beatings that almost killed him. Even then he secretly heard confessions and spoke to the other prisoners about God's love. When food was brought in, he stepped aside for the others. Sometimes there was nothing left for him. Once, when he was asked why he did this, his answer was, "I want to give my life for the good of all people."

One day a prisoner escaped from the camp. As a result, the officers said ten men must die by starvation in an underground pit. The guards chose ten men to die. One man cried out, "My wife, my children! I shall never see them again!" Another prisoner stepped forward and offered to take his place. It was Father Kolbe, prisoner 16670.

While they were in the pit, Father Kolbe led the nine men in prayer and song to Mary, God's mother. It sounded like a church full of people. No one had heard anything like it in prison before. Father Kolbe prayed and suffered bravely as Jesus did. He gave his life for another, and he lifted the spirits of the other nine men who died.

After his death the news of Father Kolbe's great love spread to the whole world. In 1982 he was canonized. We celebrate this saint's feast day on August 14. Pope John Paul II said of Father Kolbe, "He won a victory of love. He loved both his fellow prisoners and those who put him to death. There is no greater love than this."

How did Father Kolbe live the Mass?

He sacrifie his life

Things to Do at Home

1. It has been a custom since Old Testament times to tithe. This means to give one-tenth of all your money to support the work of the Church. Figure out what this would mean for you. Pray and ask God what he wants you to give to the Church and ask him to help you to be generous. Prepare an envelope for next Sunday's offering.

2. Study Eucharistic Prayers II and III in an old missalette.
   - ✣ Place a box around the words of Jesus at the Last Supper.
   - ✣ Place a straight line under the words offering Jesus to his Father.
   - ✣ Place a wavy line under the words of the acclamation.
   - ✣ Place a colored box around the Great Amen.

3. Renew yourself in praying the Morning Offering on the inside front cover of this book. In this prayer you offer your day in union with the Holy Sacrifice of the Mass throughout the world.

We Remember

What do we do in the Eucharistic Prayer?
In the Eucharistic Prayer we thank and praise God for the works of salvation. We join ourselves with Jesus as he offers himself to his Father.

Words to Know
Preface
consecration
memorial acclamation
Great Amen

We Respond

I will offer a sacrifice of thanksgiving and call on the name of the LORD.
Psalm 116:17

We Review

A Miracle   Though our eyes do not see it, Jesus uses his power to work a great miracle at every Mass. Decode the message that tells what it is. Write the letter of the alphabet that comes before the one given.

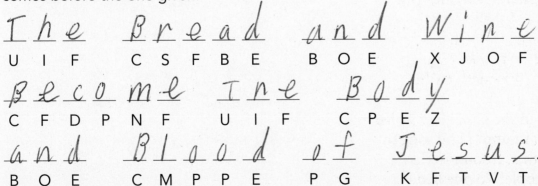

The   Bread   and   Wine
UIF   CSFBE   BOE   XJOF

Become   The   Body
CFDPNF   UIF   CPEZ

and   Blood   of   Jesus.
BOE   CMPPE   PG   KFTVT

Order of Events   Number these parts of the Liturgy of the Eucharist in the order in which they happen.

_4_ Narrative of the Last Supper

_3_ Holy, Holy, Holy

_2_ Preface

_6_ Great Amen

_1_ community presentation of gifts

_5_ acclamation proclaiming the mystery of our faith

Pairs   Fill in the blanks. The first letters of the missing words are given.

B_read_ and w_ine_ become Jesus at Mass.

Jesus is the perfect sacrifice: he is both G_od_ and

m_an_ .

We celebrate the Eucharist to p_raise_ and t_hank_ God.

During the Eucharist we offer God J_esus_ and

o_urselves_ .

Responses   Go through this chapter and underline your words during the Liturgy of the Eucharist. How many responses did you underline?

_____

Jesus Gives Himself to Us

Often the members of a family are so busy that there is no time during the day when they are all together. But certain days, like birthdays, are so special that everyone wants to be home to celebrate, especially at dinnertime.

When we eat together, we are sharing the food that gives us life. Through mealtime conversation, we are also sharing our joys and sorrows. We pray together, asking God to bless us and our food. All of these things help us to know and love one another more.

The Eucharist is a special meal. We come together as the Christian community to be fed with the Bread of Life and the cup of salvation. We come to Mass to receive Jesus, the Father's gift to us.

Jesus comes to us with his life and love in Holy Communion. Communion means "union with." When we receive Jesus in this sacrament, we come into a special and holy union with God. We are united more closely with one another too. Together we pray with Jesus to the Father. We praise and thank God for the gift of his Son, Jesus, and for all his gifts. We ask Jesus for the grace we need to love one another as he loves us. We ask him to help us witness to him and serve the Church.

Because the Eucharist makes us one with Jesus and one another, it is the sacrament of unity. A Church law requires that we receive Holy Communion at least once a year during the Easter season.

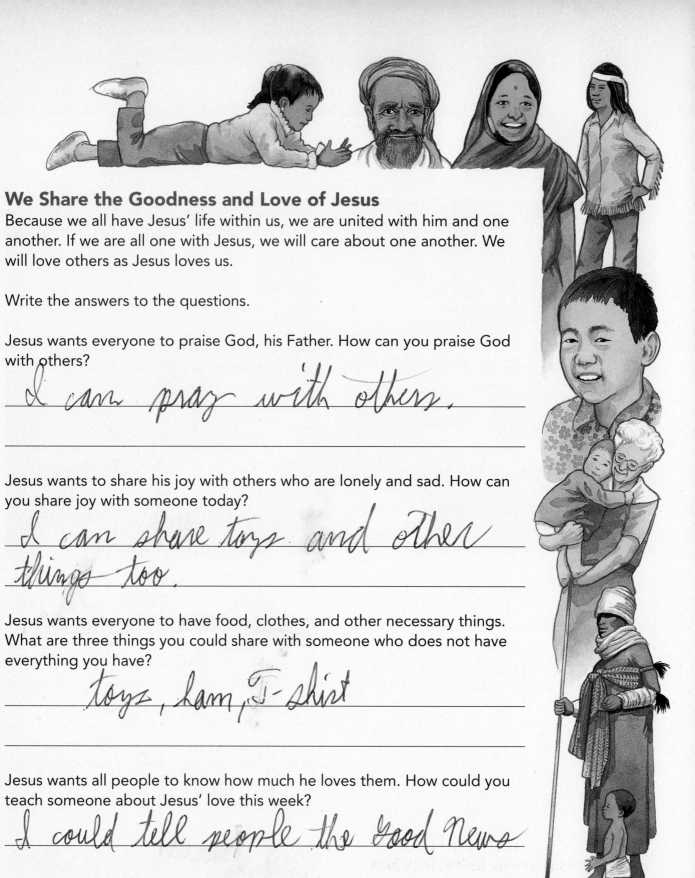

We Share the Goodness and Love of Jesus

Because we all have Jesus' life within us, we are united with him and one another. If we are all one with Jesus, we will care about one another. We will love others as Jesus loves us.

Write the answers to the questions.

Jesus wants everyone to praise God, his Father. How can you praise God with others?

I can pray with others.

Jesus wants to share his joy with others who are lonely and sad. How can you share joy with someone today?

I can share toys and other things too.

Jesus wants everyone to have food, clothes, and other necessary things. What are three things you could share with someone who does not have everything you have?

toys, ham, T-shirt

Jesus wants all people to know how much he loves them. How could you teach someone about Jesus' love this week?

I could tell people the Good News

Yes, Jesus shares his life and love with us. He is waiting now for us to share our lives and love with all our brothers and sisters, united in his love.

We Receive Jesus with Love

During the Liturgy of the Eucharist there are two processions. In the first one our gifts of bread and wine are presented to the priest. During the Eucharistic Prayer these gifts become the Body and Blood of Jesus and are offered to his Father. Then, in the Communion procession, we go to receive Jesus. How generous God is to us, his children! Father Bob will tell about this part of the Mass.

Communion Rite

Lord's Prayer

Before we share the family meal with God's people, we pray together the prayer that Jesus taught us. Two petitions in the prayer make it a perfect mealtime prayer. We ask God to give us "our daily bread." *Bread* here means all the things we need for daily life as well as the Bread of Life, the Eucharist. In the Our Father we also ask forgiveness. We want to be reconciled with God and all our brothers and sisters in Christ. Family members want to be at peace with one another at mealtime.

Sign of Peace

We ask God for the peace of Christ and then wish peace to one another. We give some **sign of peace** to people near us. What we say is like a prayer for the person (for example, "May the peace of Christ be with you"). When we offer this sign, we should think about the great love of Jesus and the peace he brings.

Breaking of the Bread

I break the bread and prepare it to be eaten. In sharing the one bread, we all receive the same food: Jesus. We are united with him and one another. While the bread is being prepared, we say or sing the **Lamb of God.** In this prayer we ask Jesus to take away the sins of the world and grant us peace.

Communion

I hold up the sacred host and say, "This is the Lamb of God who takes away the sins of the world. Happy are those who are called to his supper." You respond as the centurion in the Gospel did: "Lord, I am not worthy to receive you, but only say the word and I shall be healed." Then I receive Communion.

In the Communion procession you walk to Holy Communion as brothers and sisters going to meet the Lord Jesus. Your joyful union is shown as you join your voices in song. As you reach me (or the eucharistic minister), I hold a host before you and say, "The Body of Christ." Your response, "Amen!" ("It is true"), is an act of faith. You are also declaring that you are willing to be the Body of Christ with all who share this sacred meal.

If you receive Holy Communion under the form of wine too, the minister says, "The Blood of Christ." Again, your response, "Amen!" tells Jesus that you believe you are receiving God's greatest gift—Jesus himself—and that you are willing to give your life for others as he did.

After Communion I may sit down while a song is sung and there is quiet time for a heart-to-heart talk with Jesus. We can tell him of our love for him, ask his help, and thank him for his gifts. Jesus will speak to us too. He might tell us how we can show more love for one another.

Prayer after Communion
In your name I pray that the Eucharist will bring special blessings to us and to the Church throughout the world. Again, your response, "Amen," makes this prayer your own.

A Letter from a Friend
Imagine that you received this letter from a friend who had visited you. Read it and then think of what you might write back.

Dear _____ Tammy _____,

I enjoyed my visit with you. Thank you for taking me to your church. It was the first time I had ever gone to a Catholic church. My family doesn't ever go to church. I didn't understand some of the things you did. What did people receive when they went to the front of the church? Was it something very special? Your mom told me to stay seated. Why couldn't I go up with you? Could I go with you the next time I come?

Your friend,
Terry

Write two or three thoughts you might include in your answer.

You are not a catholic. They received the body and blood of Christ will come. Come as soon as you can. From Tammy Wen

St. John Neumann Loved Jesus in the Blessed Sacrament

Bishop John Neumann, the fourth bishop of Philadelphia, loved the Mass. He wanted all the people in his diocese to have greater faith in the Blessed Sacrament. He often asked himself, "What can I do to bring the people to Jesus in the Blessed Sacrament?"

He thought of the people back in Bohemia, where he had grown up. They had a devotion called the Forty Hours, which had been started in Rome by St. Philip Neri many years before. During this devotion the people took turns praying to Jesus in the exposed Blessed Sacrament. They did this all through the day and night for forty hours.

Bishop Neumann planned to start Forty Hours in all the churches of his diocese, but first he asked some priests how they liked the plan. To his great surprise, they were against it. Some wicked people had burned down churches. The priests were afraid that these people would dishonor Jesus in the Blessed Sacrament. After that, Bishop Neumann was afraid to go ahead with his plan.

One night after a day of hard work, Bishop Neumann fell asleep leaving a candle burning beside his letters. After a while he woke up. The candle had burned down, and some letters had caught fire.

But the letters were not completely burned. He could still read them. He knelt down to thank God that all was safe. He seemed to hear God saying, "The flames did not harm these letters. No harm will come to me in the Blessed Sacrament either. Do not be afraid to carry out your plan for the Forty Hours Devotion."

After that, Bishop Neumann met again with some priests to discuss his plan. This time he strongly urged that devotion to Jesus in the Blessed Sacrament be introduced in the churches of the diocese.

All the priests voted for it. Forty Hours was first held on a diocesan level in the United States in 1853. It was held in the Church of St. Philip Neri in Philadelphia. The people's faith in the Blessed Sacrament grew, and no harm came to any of the churches.

Today Forty Hours, or some form of it, is still held in many parishes. The days when the Blessed Sacrament is given special honor are also called Eucharistic Days. Bishop John Neumann, who began this devotion in the United States, was named a saint by the Church in 1977.

Things to Do at Home

1. Make a list of five things we do at Mass that remind us that we are united with Jesus and one another.
2. Before supper tonight explain to your family why the Lord's Prayer is a good mealtime prayer. Use it as your mealtime prayer this week.
3. Talk to your family about needy people. Some people need food. Others need someone to love them. Can you think of other needs? Think of some needy people you can help.
4. Interview two eucharistic ministers. Ask why they chose this ministry and how they feel about it now. Ask what they think about and feel like as they give Communion to people.

11-37

We Remember

Why is Holy Communion called the sacrament of unity?

Holy Communion is called the sacrament of unity because Jesus makes all who receive him one in love.

We Respond

Jesus, you have made us one. Let our love for one another draw other people into union with us.

We Review

Words What do we say . . .

to ask for the Eucharist in the Our Father? *our daily bread*

when we give a sign of peace? *May the peace of Christ be with you*

that the Lamb of God takes away? *The Lamb of God take away the sins of the world*

about ourselves, using the centurion's words? *I am not worthy*

when the eucharistic minister holds the host before us and says, "The Body of Christ"? *Amen*

to make the priest's prayers our own? *Amen*

A Prayer Write a few sentences that you might say to Jesus after receiving him in Communion. Use the ideas in the fourth paragraph on page 65.

_____

_____

_____

Introductory Rites
Liturgy of the Word
Liturgy of the Eucharist
Concluding Rite

We Are Sent in God's Name

When we are having a very good time visiting a friend, we wish the visit would not end. When we leave, we try to make the joy last. We think about it. We tell people about it. We continue doing the things we did at our friend's home.

We

* play games we enjoyed,
* tell stories we heard,
* fix the same kind of food,
* sing songs we learned, and
* try to act like our friend.

The eucharistic celebration fills us with love for Jesus and for one another. After Mass we go out and share the love of Jesus with everyone we meet.

We do that by

* being joy-filled people,
* living according to God's Word, and
* doing what Jesus did in the Eucharist.

Jesus gave himself lovingly to his Father to redeem us. When we give ourselves lovingly to help one another, we are living the Mass. Jesus taught us loving service the night he gave us the Eucharist. He washed the feet of the apostles.

If all Catholics lived the Mass and loved others as Jesus loves us, the world would soon be filled with love.

Tell some ways that you think the world would be different if all Catholics lived what they celebrate at Mass.

I will share things I will say please and thank, I won't say any thing mean.

Concluding Rite

The Concluding Rite of the Mass that Father Bob explains here is very short. The important actions of giving and receiving are completed. Filled with the life and love of Jesus, we should be eager to share all we have celebrated.

Blessing

I greet you by saying, "The Lord be with you." You answer, "And also with you." Then I bless you by calling on the Trinity and making the Sign of the Cross over you. You make the Sign of the Cross on yourself. This sign reminds us of Baptism, when we were dedicated to God.

Dismissal

Catholics call the eucharistic celebration *Mass.* This comes from a Latin word that means "to send away." After receiving God's blessing, you are sent out in peace to love and serve the Lord. You are to take his love and care to the people you meet.

Your final response is one of thanksgiving: "Thanks be to God." We are grateful for all Jesus has done for us. He has given us himself. He goes with us and helps us love and serve as he did.

Closing Song

Sometimes we end our celebration with a song. We have celebrated Christ's love as a community of faith and love. Singing our final song together reminds us that we do not go out into the world alone. We each have Jesus with us, and we also have one another. Jesus has made us one—a caring, sharing community.

Word Wheel

Use the Word Wheel to help you remember the final message the priest may give. Start with G at the top of the wheel. Print G on the first line. Skip a letter and print O on the second line. Continue in this way until all the blanks are filled. Then memorize these words.

"Go in peace to love and serve the Lord."

We Take God's Love to the World

People who are sent are missionaries. Every time we celebrate Mass, we are sent out. During Mass we unite ourselves with the offering of Jesus' perfect gift to his Father. We receive Jesus himself in Holy Communion. He gives us strength to love and care about all of our brothers and sisters and sends us out as missionaries.

Through our Baptism, Jesus calls us all to share our faith with others. He calls us to share what we have and who we are. Jesus is with us and helps us use our gifts to bring his life and love to others. He can do great things for people through us when we share.

A Young Boy Shares

Read the story of the miracle of the loaves in St. John's Gospel (John 6:1–15). Answer these questions:

What did Jesus need?

Food for the people.

Whom did Jesus ask for help?

Philip a young boy

What did the young boy give Jesus?

Two fish and five barley loaves.

What wonderful thing did Jesus do with the boy's gifts?

He fed all as much as they wanted.

What would have happened if the boy had not shared?

The people would go hungry and Jesus would not have perform the miracle.

How Can We Help Jesus?

There are people all over the world who do not know Jesus. They do not know that he loves and cares about them. Jesus asks all who have been baptized to share his love with these people. He asks us to use the gifts he has given us to help them to learn to know him.

What gifts do you have that can help other people? Write them.

I help out and I have lots of time

What wonderful things can Jesus do through you if you are willing to share your gifts? Write them.

I am willing to share my brain.

We can pray that all of our brothers and sisters will

✤ listen whenever people tell them about Jesus,
✤ see Jesus' love in the Christians who help them, and
✤ love Jesus and follow him.

We can be missionaries here at home. We can be kind and helpful to the people we meet. We can help those who work in faraway missions too. We can learn more about our brothers and sisters around the world. When we understand how they live, we will love and help them more. We can make sacrifices and give the money we save to the missions. Our prayers for the missions can bring God's blessings to them.

When you are older, Jesus may call you to leave home and work in the missions. You may work in your own country or in a foreign country.

St. Francis Xavier Helps Jesus

When Francis Xavier was a young man, he did not really think about God very much. He loved sports and was a fine dancer. Francis danced the Spanish dances of his time. He was from a rich family and liked spending money and having servants.

When he met Ignatius of Loyola, Francis began to think about how he could serve God. He finally joined Ignatius and became one of the first priests in the Society of Jesus. The priests were called Jesuits. They promised to go wherever the pope would send them. *Ignatius founded the Society of Jesus*

Francis was eager to go where people did not know Jesus. He wanted to tell them about God's great love for them. Finally,

a missionary was needed to go to India. Ignatius sent Francis to "Set all afire!" Francis' heart was on fire with love, and he could hardly hide his joy.

After a trip of thirteen months, Francis arrived in India. Quickly he began to do the work of Jesus. In the mornings he visited hospitals and prisons. Afternoons were for the children. He taught them about Jesus and Jesus' teachings. Evenings were spent visiting families who needed to know Christ better. Francis spent most of the night praying. He usually got only two or three hours of sleep.

In one of his letters, Francis wrote about the people. Many did not become Christians only because there was no one to teach them. Francis told Christians about their duty to use their talents for God's kingdom.

Francis spent ten hard years in India and other countries in the Far East. Nowhere was too far. Nothing was too hard for him when there were people who did not know or love God. He traveled from India to many islands and then on to Japan. His final goal

was China, but he died of a fever while waiting to enter China. He was on an island from which he could see his beloved China. He had no priest or friend with him. He had Christ in his heart, however, so he had everything he needed.

St. Francis Xavier is a patron saint of missionaries. We can ask him to pray that we too will help those who do not know of God's great love.

Things to Do at Home

1. Make a word wheel for each member of your family. (See page 72.) Distribute the word wheels at breakfast and explain that there is a message on the wheel that will help everyone to have a happy week.
2. Look around your house for mission magazines. Bring them to class and make a mission shelf. Read at least one article about missionaries.
3. Read the story of a great missionary, such as Frances Xavier Cabrini, Isaac Jogues, or Peter Claver. Tell what gifts he or she offered to God and how God used the gifts.

We Remember

What does Jesus send us to do when we leave the eucharistic celebration?
Jesus sends us to love and serve our brothers and sisters all over the world.

We Respond

Lord, what do you wish me to do? Send me wherever you wish.

We Review

Mission Message   Use the pictures to read the sentences.

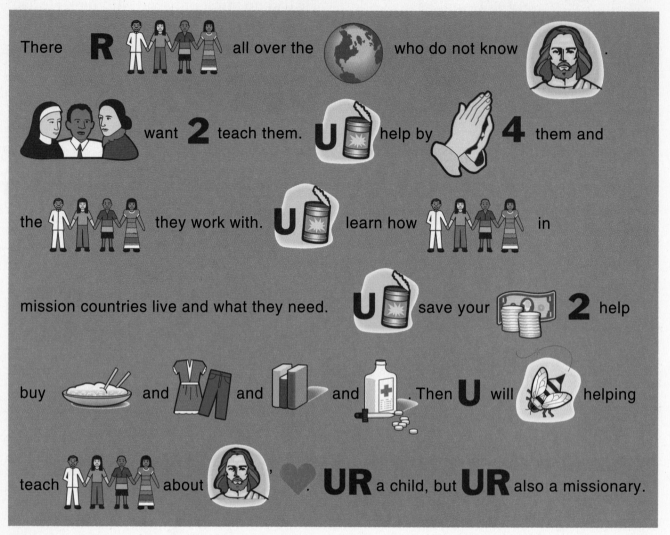

There **R** [people] all over the [globe] who do not know [Jesus].

[missionaries] want **2** teach them. **U** [can] help by [praying] **4** them and

the [people] they work with. **U** [can] learn how [people] in

mission countries live and what they need. **U** [can] save your [money] **2** help

buy [food] and [clothes] and [books] and [medicine]. Then **U** will [bee] helping

teach [people] about [Jesus]. ♥ **UR** a child, but **UR** also a missionary.

Living the Mass   Fill in the missing words.

To live the Mass means

to _____ *love* _____ as Jesus loves us.

to _____ *give* _____ ourselves to help one another.

The word _____ *Mass* _____ is from a word that means "to send away."

Right before we are sent out we receive a _____ *Blessing* _____.

_____ *God* _____ is with us to help us live the Mass.

We are called _____ *missionaries* because we are sent out.

We Celebrate the Eucharist in Memory of Jesus

12

Responding to Our Lord

Find the correct words in the smoke from the censer and complete the sentences.

General Intercessions

Liturgy of the Word

Eucharistic Prayer

Communion

Praise to you, Lord Jesus Christ.

missions

1. We listen to the readings at Mass in the _____ .
2. After the Gospel we praise Christ truly present in his Word when we say _____ .
3. After the Profession of Faith we ask God to provide for the needs of his people in the _____ .
4. We offer ourselves, our thanks, and our gifts with Jesus in the _____ .
5. We have a heart-to-heart talk with Jesus after _____ .
6. We serve others all over the world when we help the _____ .

Answer in your own words.

Liturgy of the Word

Praise to you, Lord Jesus Christ

General Intercession

Eucharistic Prayer

Communion

missions

In what ways can we show love and service to others?

I can share money.

Skywriting Puzzle
Use the words in the sky to work the puzzle.

Skywriting the Message

PEACE
EUCHARIST
SACRIFICE
CROSS
GOSPEL
LAMB
BREAD
HOMILY
THANKS

Crossword answers filled in:
1. Gospel
2. sacrifice
3. lamb
4. peace
5. bread
6. thanks
7. cross
8. homily
9. Eucharist

Across
1. The Good News is the _Gospel_
4. We offer a sign of _peace_ to show we are one.
5. Jesus took _Bread_ and said, "This is my Body."
8. In the _homily_ the priest or deacon explains the readings.
9. The sacrament in which we receive Jesus is the _Eucharist_

Down
2. In the Mass we offer ourselves with Jesus' perfect _sacrifice_
3. Jesus is called the _lamb_ of God, who takes away our sins.
6. At the Last Supper, Jesus gave _thanks_ and praise.
7. Christ gave himself for us on the _cross_

Praising the Lord

Unscramble the letters and write the missing word on the line.

1. When the Scripture is proclaimed at Mass we (SINETL) _listen_ to learn what God is asking of us.

2. In the (OIYHLM) _homily_ the priest or deacon tells us how we can live God's teaching.

3. When we recite the Profession of (THAFI) _Faith_, we tell everyone we believe in Jesus and all he teaches through the Catholic Church.

4. Jesus' gift of himself gives God perfect (ASIREP) _Praise_ and (HSNTAK) _Thanks_.

5. We give thanks by (FIORFGNE) _Offering_ ourselves to the Father with Jesus.

6. (MOINCMONU) _Communion_ unites us with Jesus and one another.

7. After Mass we go out to love and (RSEVE) _Serve_ others in the name of Jesus.

Prayers and Actions of the Mass

Under each heading, number the parts of the Mass in proper order.

Introductory Rites

__4__ Opening Prayer

__1__ Entrance Procession

__2__ Penitential Rite

__3__ Glory to God

Liturgy of the Word

__5__ Homily

__6__ Profession of Faith

__1__ First Reading

__3__ Alleluia

__2__ Responsorial Psalm

__7__ General Intercessions

__4__ Gospel

Liturgy of the Eucharist

__4__ Institution Narrative

__5__ Lord's Prayer

__7__ Communion

__6__ Sign of Peace

__1__ Preparation of the Gifts

__3__ Holy, Holy, Holy

__2__ Preface

Concluding Rite

__2__ Dismissal

__1__ Blessing

Looking Back at Unit 2

In this unit you have learned about the greatest act of worship. It is offering ourselves with Jesus, the perfect gift, in the Sacrifice of the Mass. Before we do this we prepare ourselves for it. We participate wholeheartedly in the Introductory Rites. In the Liturgy of the Word, we listen to God speak to us.

We begin the Liturgy of the Eucharist by presenting gifts of bread and wine. During the Eucharistic Prayer we praise God and give him thanks. Then Jesus becomes present under the forms of bread and wine. Together we proclaim the mystery of faith.

We offer ourselves with Jesus to the Father. We join with the priest in prayers for all the members of the Church, both the living and the dead. We give our all-important response to the Eucharistic Prayer when we say, "Amen."

God accepts our sacrifice and, in return, gives us Jesus in Holy Communion. We are full of joy as we thank and praise him. We take him with us as we go out to love and serve one another.

Living the Message

Can you give yourself a check (✓) for each statement?

❏ 1. I prepare for Mass by being quiet and by thinking about what will take place.
❏ 2. I listen to the readings at Mass to hear a message from God.
❏ 3. I offer myself with Jesus to the Father at the Eucharist.
❏ 4. I try to receive Holy Communion each time I go to Mass.
❏ 5. I praise, love, and thank Jesus after Holy Communion.

Planning to Grow

Think about Jesus' offering of himself for you on the cross and in the Eucharist. Then write three ways you plan to live the Mass.

I plan to live the Mass by saying good things. I can praise and love and thank Jesus. I can teach people about Jesus.

FAMILY FEATURE

An Original Nativity Scene

Each Advent the Garcia family from Guatemala carries out a custom practiced by many people in Mexico and Central America. The family makes its own nativity scene and displays it. The Garcias put the same scene together during Advent, assembling it piece by piece in the picture window of their home.

Each family member makes a figure out of clay, paper, or cardboard or provides a plastic one. The figures of the Christ Child, Mary, and St. Joseph are always made first—but the infant's figure is added last, on Christmas Eve. Then figures from the Old and New Testaments are added. Sometimes figures representing the family members themselves are made, as well as animals.

You might introduce this custom into your family. Decide what form your nativity scene will take. Divide up the work among the weeks of Advent. You might write on slips of paper the names of the figures you would like, put the slips into a box, and then have each family member draw out one slip to determine who is responsible for making each figure. Be creative in making the background scenery. Working together on a family nativity scene is an excellent way to prepare for the coming of Jesus Christ.

Answer these questions with your family:

✢ What is your favorite part of Mass?

family

✢ What is the most important part of Mass?

Consecration

✢ What is the saddest part of Mass?

Take this in the memore in me

✢ What is the liveliest part of Mass?

Glory to God

✢ What is the most educational part of Mass?

homily

✢ What is the quietest part of Mass?

Consecration

✢ What is the most social part of Mass?

Kiss of Peace

✢ What is a good homily that you remember?

Happy Feet

✢ How can you be an active participant in your parish Mass?

Resond

Prove It!

Prove that the Mass is . . .

- a meal: because I receive the body and body of Jesus
- a sacrament: because Jesus on Holy Thursday instituted Holy Eucharist
- a prayer: because we make the Sign of The Cross
- a celebration: because I sing songs.
- a sacrifice: because Jesus sacrificed himself

Word Search

In the space below, see how many words you can make out of the word *Eucharist*. Use each letter only as many times as it occurs in the word *Eucharist*.

such are eat each car
star tar share air
care I chair use chest
heart heat cheat itch the hair
harsh tear hit his hate use
react act christ is at rats charts
teach star reach sit rich ears east
rise Eric Irish cats hers

We Celebrate God's Healing Love

Sacraments of Healing

You have learned about the sacraments of initiation, which make us members of God's family. Baptism, Confirmation, and the Eucharist fill us with grace and help us live like Jesus. The Sacrament of the Eucharist nourishes and strengthens us. But what happens if we harm our life in Christ? How can it be renewed? In this unit you will study the sacraments Jesus has provided for our spiritual (and sometimes bodily) healing: the Sacrament of Reconciliation (Penance) and the Anointing of the Sick.

God Enables Us to Make Right Choices

Every day we make many choices. Some are not important, and we do not notice them. Others are so serious that they may change our lives.

God has given us the freedom to make choices. Sometimes we make a wrong choice. We choose what looks good, and it turns out to be bad. Sometimes we purposely choose the wrong thing. In any case, we are responsible for our choices and their results. If you choose to eat too much candy and get sick, you can blame no one but yourself. If you choose to cross the street before the traffic stops, you are responsible if an accident happens.

My Choices

Think back on a poor choice you have made. How did you feel about it afterward? Think about a good choice you made. How did you feel about it? Write about your choices here.

A poor choice I made was _when I chose to hit someone._

I felt _really bad_

A good choice I made was _when I chose to help my mom_

I felt _good_

How can we make right choices? As persons, we have the gift of **conscience,** through which God speaks. With this gift, we are able to know what is right or wrong. We can judge what choices we should make.

We are free to choose either right or wrong, but as baptized Christians we want to follow Christ. To do this we must work to form a right conscience. Then it will help us to judge correctly what is right and what is wrong. We should always follow our consciences and do what we know is right.

God has given us guides for judging right and wrong. They are his commandments, Scripture, and the teachings of Jesus and his Church. Any choice made according to these guides will be a good one.

Other helps in forming a right conscience:

- parents and other family members
- good friends and other good people
- priests, deacons, brothers, and sisters
- good experiences we have had
- good books we have read
- Mary and the saints
- prayer and the sacraments
- the study of our religion
- having a good relationship with God

If we use the helps God has given us, we are better able to form good consciences that can judge what is right and what is wrong. We will be able to judge according to reason and recognize the good that God wants us to do. Most important, God will help us if we ask. He will give us the grace to choose what is right and the courage to do it.

The Roads of Choice

What helps have you used to make the right choices? Print four of them on the signs along Good Choice Road. Which road would you take?

Christ's Forgiving Love Heals Us

Some two thousand years ago, Jesus gave his life to save all people from the death brought about by sin. What a great price he paid so that we could live forever! Scripture says:

> You were ransomed from your futile conduct . . . not with perishable things like silver or gold but with the precious blood of Christ.
>
> 1 Peter 1:18–19

From the sufferings and death of Jesus, an innocent man, we can see how terrible sin is. How great his sufferings were in the scourging, the crowning with thorns, and his crucifixion. His enemies executed him and his friends left him. In obedience to his Father, Jesus redeemed us from sin and death. How evil sin must be if it cost Jesus so much!

Violence, war, hatred, jealousy, selfishness, death, and other evils are all around us. The sins we commit bring unhappiness to ourselves and others in the human family.

We commit **sin** when we know what God wants us to do and yet we freely choose to disobey him. We disobey God when we do something against his law of love or omit doing something good. Sin can be committed by thoughts, words, actions, or omissions.

I omit doing the good

Study

Mortal sin cuts us off from God's friendship completely. We cannot commit this sin without knowing it. We commit mortal sin when *memorize*

✢ we do something *seriously wrong;*

✢ we *know* it is seriously wrong;

✢ we *freely and willingly choose* it.

If we have committed a mortal sin, we must be truly sorry for it and confess it in the Sacrament of Reconciliation.

Venial sin weakens our friendship with God but does not cut us off completely from him. The sin is evil, but not so serious as a mortal sin. Venial sins can be forgiven by praying an Act of Contrition, by receiving the Eucharist, or by performing good works. It is good to confess venial sins because they can become a habit and lead to mortal sin.

As good Christians we try to avoid all sin. If we do fail and commit sin, Christ will always give us the grace to return to God our Father. Jesus loves sinners and wants all people to share in his joy. As he forgave sinners when he lived on earth, Jesus forgives us today. In the **Sacrament of Reconciliation** he forgives all sins, mortal or venial, when we are truly sorry and promise to sin no more. In this sacrament we are healed, saved, and made new again by Christ's merciful love. We are made stronger in God's love and grace.

Things to Do at Home

1. Share with your family what you have learned about making good choices. Talk over ways of choosing good television programs to watch. Decide what you will do if the choice that has been made turns out to be a poor one.

2. Get into the habit of making a short Act of Contrition at certain times. You might say it before going to bed or before you go on a trip. You might say it when you realize you have done something wrong or when you are in danger. A good one to say is "Lord Jesus Christ, Son of God, have mercy on me, a sinner."

Study We Remember

What is sin?

Sin is choosing to disobey God. It is mortal when the action is seriously wrong, we know it is wrong, and we do it freely and willingly. Venial sin is less serious.

What is conscience?

Conscience is the power to judge what is right and wrong.

Words to Know

conscience   venial sin
mortal sin

Words to Memorize
An Act of Contrition

We Respond

Lord Jesus Christ, Son of God, have mercy on me, a sinner.

We Review

Healing Love Puzzle   Write the correct answers on the lines of the puzzle.

God gives us freedom to *choose*

A less serious sin is called *venial*.

A serious sin, knowingly and willingly committed, is called *mortal*

A gift that helps us judge right and wrong is *conscience*

We are *responsible* for our choices.

Grace enables us to make right choices.

C H O O S E
V E N I A L
M O R T A L
    L ♥ V E
C O N S C I E N C E
R E S P O N S I B L E
   G R A C E

God's Guides   Fill in the vowels.

What helps in forming a right conscience has God given us?

the c _o_ mm _a_ ndm _e_ nts

the t _e_ _a_ ch _i_ ngs of J _e_ s _u_ s and h _i_ s Ch _u_ rch

Jesus Invites Us to Change Our Hearts

Did you ever go to a parade or a ball game where you were not able to see? The people in front of you were just too tall! Some adults have this problem. In the Gospel of Luke 19:1–10, we read a wonderful story about a man named Zacchaeus who wanted to see Jesus. Although Zacchaeus was short and could not see above the crowd, he found a way to see Jesus. Even more important, Jesus saw him.

As Jesus was walking down a road in Jericho, a crowd gathered. Zacchaeus the tax collector was among them. How the Jews hated tax collectors, who took their money for Rome! Tax collectors usually took even more than Rome wanted. The extra money went into their own pockets, and they soon became rich.

Zacchaeus was one of the most important tax collectors. He was very rich! He was also very clever. When he couldn't see over the people's heads, he ran ahead and climbed up into a sycamore tree. He was ready. He could see everything that was going on.

When Jesus reached the spot by the tree, he looked up at Zacchaeus. He loved Zacchaeus and wanted to tell him so. He spoke with great respect and asked Zacchaeus to hurry down. He said he wanted to stay at Zacchaeus's house.

Zacchaeus was surprised! His heart was touched! There were many other people there, but Jesus wanted to come to his house. Zacchaeus knew Jesus loved him, and he loved Jesus in return. His heart was

changed by Jesus' love. Zacchaeus saw the evil things he had done. He knew why the other Jews hated him, and he wanted to change his life. He wanted to show his love to Jesus, so he began right away. "I am going to give half of my property to the poor," he told Jesus. "If I have cheated anybody I will pay back four times the amount." How happy Jesus was as he told Zacchaeus, "Today salvation has come to this house."

Jesus is looking for us wherever we are. He is waiting for us to come to him and listen to him. Jesus wants to touch us and heal us from sin. If we are watching for him, Jesus will speak to our hearts. He will let us know that he loves us and wants to be with us. We will want to change our lives and do what he tells us. We will be filled with **contrition,** sorrow for sin.

Like Zacchaeus we can find a place where we can meet Jesus. Ordinary sins are forgiven through the Eucharist. We can meet Jesus in a special way, however, in the Sacrament of Reconciliation. In this sacrament Jesus tells us of his forgiving love. He wants to change our hearts so that we can live with him forever. He wants to take away our sins and fill our hearts with love. He wants us to let him forgive us.

Knowing Jesus loves us, we can admit that we have sinned. Jesus loves us even though we are sinners. He wants to heal our weakness and help us grow strong in love. We are sorry for our sins and confess them because we love Jesus. We promise to keep trying to become holy. Being sorry for love of God is perfect contrition.

As we come to know how much Jesus loves us, we want to be more like him. We want to give up those things that have kept us away from him. We want to give up our selfishness and share all that we have with others. We want to be kind to those we have hurt. We want to be obedient to those we have disobeyed. Like Zacchaeus we try to make up for hurtful things we have done.

Making Up
How could you make up . . .

for writing on the wall at school?

I would offer to clean the wall

for starting a rumor that a person in your class was shoplifting?

I would defend him and say it is not true

for your younger brother's breaking his leg because you went off while you were supposed to be watching him?

I would help him in any way.

When we receive the Sacrament of Reconciliation, we show Jesus our love. Saying "I'm sorry" and asking forgiveness are signs of our love. Giving forgiveness is also a sign of love. Just as Jesus always forgives us, we must forgive one another. When it is hard to ask someone to forgive us or to forgive another, we can remember how much Jesus loves us and ask him to help us. How Jesus must rejoice each time he can say to us in this sacrament, as he said to Zacchaeus, "Today salvation has come to this house"!

St. Paul Apostle "To the Gentiles"

Jesus Gives the Gift of Peace

According to the Gospel of John, Jesus gave us the gift of the Sacrament of Reconciliation on Easter Sunday night. The disciples were gathered behind locked doors when Jesus appeared to them. He gave them peace and then enabled them to bring his peace to others. He breathed on them and said,

"Receive the holy Spirit. Whose sins you forgive are forgiven them, and whose sins you retain are retained."

John 20:22

The way in which Christ's forgiveness is given to Christians has changed through the centuries. Today we may celebrate the sacrament privately. We may also participate in a communal (community) celebration, which prepares us to confess our sins and receive absolution individually.

We Meet Jesus in Reconciliation

Every hiker knows the importance of a compass. It is not something to be packed in the bottom of the supply bag. Rather, it must be kept at hand and used again and again. Checking a compass helps the hiker to be sure of going the right way.

The Sacrament of Reconciliation helps us to be sure we are on our way to God our Father. Jesus has gone before us and marked the trail. He wants to take us to his Father. But when we move slowly, or go off the trail by sinning, we need the help of the Sacrament of Reconciliation. When we wander, Jesus is patient. He waits for us in this sacrament. A good hiker must know how to use a compass before going hiking. We need to know how

to meet Jesus in this sacrament if we are to walk with him to our Father.

The Church knows how important and how helpful it is to receive this sacrament. For this reason the Church has made it a precept (law) that Catholics must confess their sins at least once a year.

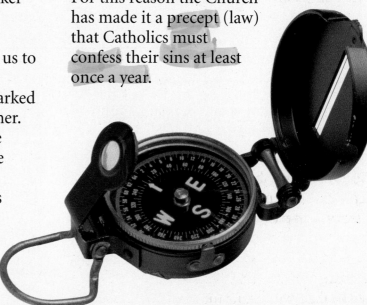

Steps to Reconciliation

Make sentences out of the following mixed-up groups of words, and you will have the six steps to follow when you celebrate the Sacrament of Reconciliation.

1. Pray the Spirit to Holy _Pray to the Holy Spirit._

2. love God's forgiving of Think _Think of God's forgiving love._

3. your Examine conscience _Examine your conscience._

4. Act of Pray an Contrition _Pray an Act of Contrition._

5. your the priest sins to Confess _Confess your sins to the priest._

6. love Thank for God his forgiving _Thank God for his forgiving love._

Preparing

God loves us and wants us to be happy forever. Jesus has made a path to lead us safely to God and perfect happiness. He has given us his Holy Spirit to help us follow his way of love. To prepare for the Sacrament of Reconciliation, we **pray to the Holy Spirit.** We ask the Spirit to show us how we have loved or failed to love. We ask the Spirit to be with us and help us as we celebrate this sacrament.

God speaks to us in his holy Word. God often talks about forgiveness because he is waiting to show forgiving love to every sinner. God's Word tells us that he loves us and is waiting to forgive us.

We **examine our consciences** to see how we have walked with Jesus on the path of love. Have we followed in his footsteps at home, at school, and elsewhere? Have we loved God, ourselves, and others?

We **tell God we are sorry,** and we **promise to try to be more loving,** more like Jesus. We want to change our ways and renew our baptismal covenant.

Confessing

We decide what we will tell the priest when we confess our sins. Anyone who has completely turned from God by committing mortal sin must tell that sin in confession. Children usually commit venial sins. They will confess the sins they commit most often, or the sins that hurt others the most. When we **confess our sins,** we tell the priest how we have failed in love and more or less how often. It is also good to tell the reason, if we know it.

Ben often cheated in school. He decided to confess his sin this way: "I cheat in almost every test at school because I like to get good grades the way my friend Joe does."

Amelia was unkind to her younger brothers and sisters. This is the way she confessed her sin: "I'm unkind and yell at my younger brothers and sisters often because they always play while I work."

Do you know the answers to these questions? Write them on the lines.

Cara tells many lies. Can you think of a reason boys or girls your age tell lies?

_____

_____

How might Cara confess this sin?

_____

_____

Russell makes fun of Kenny, who never learned to play soccer. Why might he be doing this?

_____

_____

How could he confess this sin?

_____

_____

Receiving a Penance

After we confess our sins, the priest talks to us. He gives us a **penance**—something that will help us keep our promise to be better. This may be either a prayer to say or something good to do. It is a sign that we want to make up for our sins. Sometimes the priest may ask us what we think would be a good penance. We do our penance as soon as possible so that we don't forget it.

Think what might be good penances for the children you just met. Write a penance that would be a sign they want to make up for their sins.

Ben _should study a lot for the test._

Amelia _You should ask them to play somewhere else._

Cara _to avoid punishment or to seem important. Cara spend some time asking Jesus to tell the truth._

Russell _he want to look good himself or he doesn't like kenny. Father I don't like kenny. Russell help him play soccer._

Receiving Forgiveness

Then comes the most wonderful part of the sacrament. We tell Jesus we are sorry in an **Act of Contrition.** Then Jesus forgives our sins through the words and actions of the priest. The priest extends his hand over us and gives us **absolution.** He says, "I absolve you from your sins in the name of the Father, and of the Son, † and of the Holy Spirit." As he says this, we make the Sign of the Cross.

Celebrating the Sacrament

When I am ready to celebrate the Sacrament of Reconciliation, I go to meet Jesus. I meet him through the priest who acts in his name and in the name of the whole Church.

Welcome by the Priest
1. He greets me warmly.
2. I make the Sign of the Cross with the priest.
3. The priest invites me to trust in God.

Reading God's Word
The priest may read from the Bible, or I may read a passage that I have chosen.

Confessing My Sins and Accepting Penance
1. I tell my sins. I tell those things that keep me from being the kind of person Jesus expects me to be.
2. I listen as the priest tells me how I can be that kind of person. He explains how I can love God more by bringing his love and goodness into my world. I can also ask the priest questions.
3. The priest gives me a penance.

Prayer of Sorrow and Absolution
1. I pray an Act of Contrition, really thinking about what I am saying.
2. The priest gives me God's forgiveness and reconciles me with God and the Church. The priest prays a prayer and gives me absolution. I say, "Amen."

Praise of God and Dismissal
1. The priest says, "Give thanks to the Lord, for he is good." I say, "His mercy endures forever."
2. The priest may say, "The Lord has freed you from your sins. Go in peace."
3. I express my thanks to God and the priest.

Things to Do at Home

1. Find out when the Sacrament of Reconciliation is celebrated in your parish church. You might arrange to go to confession as a family.

2. Look through Luke 7:36–50 and Luke 15. Draw a picture of your favorite story about God's forgiving love. Put the picture where you say your night prayers. When you see it, pray your Act of Contrition.

3. Briefly examine your conscience every night as a preparation for the Sacrament of Reconciliation.

4. Write a story about someone your age who does something wrong, is sorry, and makes up for it.

We Remember

What does Jesus do for us in the Sacrament of Reconciliation?
In the Sacrament of Reconciliation, Jesus forgives our sins. He brings us into a closer union with himself, one another, and the whole Church.

Words to Know
contrition   absolution
penance

We Respond

Forgive us our trespasses as we forgive those who trespass against us.

We Review *Study*

A Change of Heart   Read the verse and answer the question.

> I will give them a new heart and put a new spirit
>   within them.
>   Ezekiel 11:19

How did Zacchaeus receive a new heart?

Zacchaeus was sorry for his sin and decided to give back to those he cheated.

> Though your sins be like scarlet,
>   they may become white as snow.
>   Isaiah 1:18

How can your worst sins be changed?

My worst sins can be changed threw Jesus' forgivness and saying sorry.

The Keys to the Kingdom   Keys are a symbol of the Sacrament of Reconciliation. Use the words in the keys to answer the questions.

absolution

contrition

peace

mortal

priest

Easter

penance

1. Who represents Christ and the Church in forgiving sin?   *priest*

2. On what night did Jesus give us the gift of the Sacrament of Reconciliation?   *Easter*

3. What does Jesus give us in the Sacrament of Reconciliation?   *peace*

4. What kind of sins separate a person completely from God and must be confessed?   *mortal*

5. What do we call the words said to forgive sin?   *absolution*

6. What is the most important thing we must have in order to be forgiven?   *contrition*

7. What are prayers or deeds that help us change our lives and show that we want to make up for our sin?   *penance*

95

The Sick Need Special Help

When we really care about people, we are interested in what happens to them. We are concerned about how they feel. If they are happy, we rejoice with them. If they are sick or suffering, we do things to help them feel better.

Many Gospel stories tell us how Jesus healed people of every kind of disease and sickness. Name three things Jesus did to help sick or suffering people.

Jesus gave sight to Bartimaus

Jesus helped lepers.

Jesus healed the paralytic people.

Sickness and suffering are a mystery. Sometimes we wonder why God permits them. Sickness is an evil that makes people suffer and struggle to overcome special handicaps. The sick are weak and may even find it hard to pray.

God can bring good out of evil if we trust him. Our God is a God of love. He created us because he loves us. God calls us to have life in him. He sent his Son Jesus into the world so that we could

have everlasting life. God uses everything that happens to us, even sickness and suffering, to bring us closer to him.

Through the prophet Isaiah, God tells us we can say,

> God indeed is my savior;
>   I am confident and unafraid.
> My strength and my courage is
>   the LORD.
>
> Isaiah 12:2

We trust in God's love for us. We believe that God will lead us through sickness or suffering to a happier, better life.

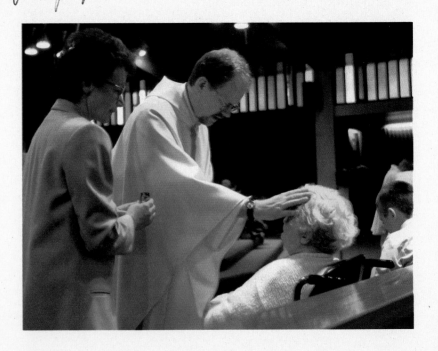

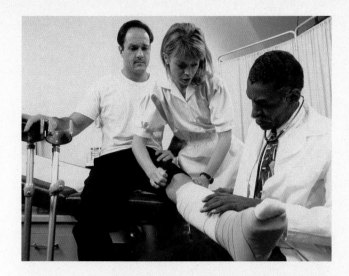

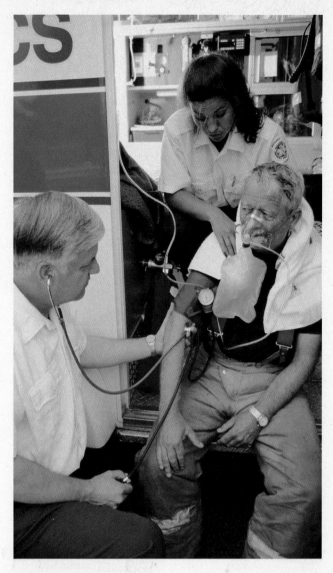

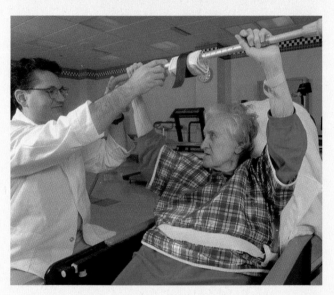

When people are sick or in pain, they need special care. They need someone to help them. Doctors, nurses, and other health-care providers devote themselves to caring for the sick. All Christians help the sick by praying for them and giving them loving care. Whenever we care for the sick and suffering, we are doing the healing work of Jesus.

We Help the Sick
Can you think of two things you could do to care for the sick?
Write them here.

I can pray for them. I can be their messagers.

Jesus Heals in the Anointing of the Sick

Jesus does not cure the sick simply to take away their suffering. He cures them to help them believe and trust in him. When he does not cure them, he helps them accept their sickness as he accepted his cross. Even the greatest sufferings are small when compared to the glory that God has waiting for us. God wants us to trust that he will permit only what can lead us to that glory.

The sick and the aged need God's help to be able to suffer patiently with faith and love. The Church brings Christ's love and support in the Sacrament of the Anointing of the Sick. Through the sacrament's power to take away sins, health is restored to the soul. The sacrament sometimes restores health to the body.

These members of the Church may receive the Anointing of the Sick:

✢ those who are dangerously ill
✢ the elderly, who are weak
✢ those about to have serious surgery

People may be anointed more than once. They should ask to celebrate this sacrament whenever they become seriously ill.

The Anointing of the Sick may be celebrated in church, a person's home, a hospital, or a nursing home. It may be celebrated outside Mass or during Mass after the homily. The family and friends of sick people should be with them at the anointing and should pray for them.

Those who celebrate the sacrament trust that Jesus will comfort them. They are helped to accept their sufferings as their share in Christ's suffering.

Lord, make me well again.

The Rite of Anointing Brings Peace

The priest begins by greeting all with peace. He then either instructs the people about the sacrament or prays that God will bless all present. The Sacrament of Reconciliation or a penitential rite is celebrated.

Readings from Scripture follow. Usually a priest will talk about the readings. He will prepare the sick for the grace God offers in the anointing.

Here or somewhere else in the ceremony the priest and everyone present pray for the person being anointed. They ask God to free him or her from sin and illness.

Then the priest lays his hands in silence on the head of the sick person.

After that he anoints the forehead and hands of the sick person with oil, praying:

Through this holy anointing
may the Lord in his love and mercy
   help you
with the grace of the Holy Spirit.
May the Lord who frees you from sin
save you and raise you up.

The anointing in the name of the Lord reminds the sick that they can trust in God's love. It comforts and strengthens them. In this sacrament the sick praise God's constant love. They remember that God guides them through suffering to a fuller life.

Next the priest asks that Jesus restore the sick person to health. Everyone prays the Our Father. Then Communion may be given to the sick person and others present. Communion given to someone who is dying is called **Viaticum.** The rite ends with a blessing by the priest for everyone.

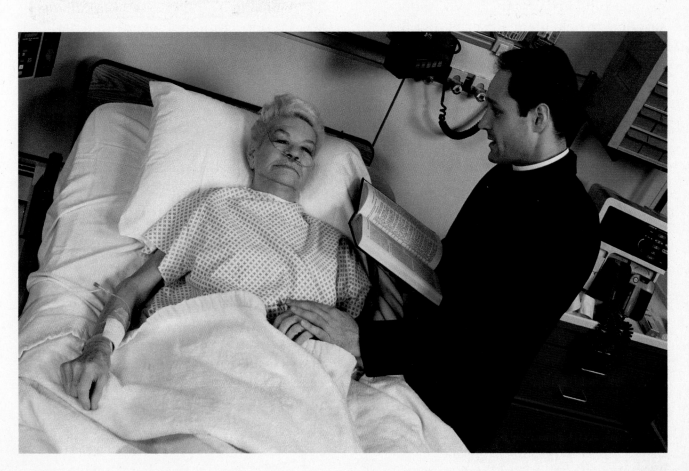

Rose Hawthorne Cared for the Sick as Jesus Did

"I am for God and the Poor"

Rose Hawthorne Lathrop borrowed this motto from a great saint who served God's poor, St. Vincent de Paul. Like him, Rose loved God and those who were sick and poor.

Rose Hawthorne Lathrop was the daughter of the great American writer Nathaniel Hawthorne. She was born in Massachusetts on May 20, 1851. By the time she was nine, Rose had lived in England and traveled to Scotland, France, and Italy. Then her family returned to America.

Rose never forgot some of the sad things she had seen in the crowded Italian cities. She felt sorry for the crippled children standing or sitting by the curbs. She wondered how people could just pass them by without stopping to help them. Rose felt that she should do something for them, but because she could think of nothing she could do, she decided just to stay away. Later on, Rose would not be able to walk away from anyone who needed help.

In 1871, when Rose was twenty, she married a fine young man named George Lathrop. They loved each other deeply, and soon they had a son. When their little boy was only five, however, he became very sick and died. How George and Rose missed him! George turned to drinking. When it was not safe for Rose to be with him, she knew she must leave him. The two separated. Now Rose was all alone. It seemed that sorrow crossed her path wherever she turned.

Rose knew that God would show her what he wanted her to do. Soon God led her to see the terrible sufferings of the poor who had cancer. There were no free beds in hospitals. The poor often died without anyone to care for them.

Rose got an idea of how to help, but her friends said her idea would never work. She did not have much money, but Rose said simply, "I can't do much, but I'll do the best I can." It was 1896 when she left her peaceful home and moved to the slums of New York City. She was sure some people would help when they saw the real needs of the sick poor.

Rose found a small place in the slums that she made into a home for cancer patients. She did not accept just anyone into her home. She took only those who could not pay for help and who would never get well.

Shortly after she began her work with the sick poor, Rose received sad news. Her husband was very ill and was asking for her. She went immediately to the hospital and heard him say, "Please forgive me." George died at peace with God and his wife. Rose was relieved. Her husband was now safe, and she could devote her life to her new work.

In 1899 Rose Hawthorne Lathrop decided to do more for the sick poor. She started a new Dominican order called Servants for the Relief of Incurable Cancer.

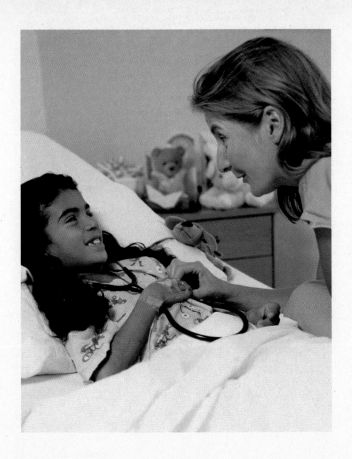

Today, the sisters in Rose's order care for cancer patients whom doctors and medicines cannot cure. The sisters do not accept any pay from their patients or their families. Generous people who have heard about their work send money. Some send clothing and cloth for bandages. Others send prayers.

Patients in the cancer homes receive the best health care. They are kept busy and happy. Thousands of the sick poor have been cared for in these homes. All have found God's loving presence and care.

There are many little things we can do to serve the sick. Draw 😊 or 🙁 to show how the sick would feel if we did what the sentence says.

Send them a get-well card.

Pray that God will heal them.

Do noisy things when you're near them.

Read them a cheerful story.

Bring them flowers or another little gift.

Let a priest know if they are seriously ill.

Tell them, "You'll never catch up on your schoolwork."

Offer to take care of something for them.

We Celebrate Our Faith in God's Power to Heal

God does wonderful things for those who believe! God never refuses help to anyone who comes to him with faith. We have come together in the name of our Lord, Jesus Christ. We pray for all the sick.

Song

Reading

Jesus Heals the Daughter of Jairus (adapted from Mark 5:21–43)

Reader 1: One day Jesus was teaching a crowd of people. Jairus, a synagogue official, came forward and fell at Jesus' feet.

Jairus: My daughter is at the point of death. Please, come lay your hands on her that she may get well and live.

Jesus: I will come.

Reader 2: Jesus went with Jairus, and the crowd followed. He stopped a while to heal a woman. While Jesus was still speaking, people from Jairus's house arrived and came up to Jairus.

Messenger: Your daughter has died. Why trouble the teacher any longer?

Jesus: Do not be afraid; just have faith.

Reader 3: When they reached the house, people were already weeping and wailing.

Jesus: Why this commotion and weeping? The child is not dead but only asleep.

Reader 4: At that, the people made fun of Jesus. He sent them out. He took Peter, James, and John, along with the girl's mother and father, to the room where the child was. He took the child by the hand.

Jesus: Little girl, I say to you, arise.

Reader 5: The girl, a child of twelve, arose immediately and walked around.

Jesus: Do not tell this to anyone. Give the girl something to eat.

Reader 5: The Gospel of the Lord.

All: Praise to you, Lord Jesus Christ.

Response

Catechist: With faith let us ask the Lord to hear our prayers for the sick and for all those who care for them.

All: Lord, hear our prayer.

Catechist: Look kindly, Lord, on all the sick and suffering people in the world. Give them patience, hope, and courage to endure their pain.

All: Lord, hear our prayer.

Catechist: You commanded the apostles to lay their hands on the sick in your name. May your people remember your saving power and turn to you in time of trouble.

All: Lord, hear our prayer.

Catechist: Lord, you comforted the sick and suffering. Assist those who continue your work of caring for them.

All: Lord, hear our prayer.

Prayer of Thanksgiving

Praise to you, almighty God and Father.
You sent your Son to live among us and bring us to salvation.

Praise to you, Lord Jesus Christ.
You loved us to the very end of your life.
You willingly accepted death that we might have life, and
you desire to cure all our illnesses.

Praise to you, God the Holy Spirit.
You heal our sickness with your mighty power.
Lord God, with faith in you we call upon your name.
We ask you to strengthen the sick and relieve their pain.
We ask this through Christ our Lord.

The Lord's Prayer

Now let us pray with confidence as our Lord, Jesus Christ, has taught us. Our Father . . .

Song

Things to Do at Home

1. Look up Mark 1:40–45 and answer the following questions:
   ⬧ Who needed help? *a leper man*
   ⬧ How was the person suffering? *he leprosy*
   ⬧ What did Jesus say? *tell no one show yourself to the priest*
   ⬧ How did the person respond? *he told everyone*
2. Tell members of your family why you would like to be anointed if you became seriously ill. Ask them how they think the Anointing of the Sick could bring all of you closer to Jesus.
3. When those you love are sick or suffering, pray for them. Do something to comfort them or cheer them up.
4. Spend some time talking with Jesus when you have pain and sorrows. Ask him to touch you with his healing love.

We Remember

How does the Sacrament of the Anointing of the Sick help the sick?
The Sacrament of the Anointing of the Sick brings health to the soul and sometimes to the body. It comforts and strengthens the sick and helps them unite their sufferings with Christ's.

> ## Word to Know
> Viaticum *Study*

We Respond

Relieve the sufferings of all the sick. Lord, hear our prayer.
Rite of the Anointing of the Sick

We Review

Ideas to Remember   Find the right ending for each sentence below. Write the letter of the ending on the line.

1. Persons who are seriously ill should __C__.
2. The Anointing of the Sick may be received __D__.
3. Everyone can care for the sick by __a__.
4. The priest who anoints the sick __B__.

A. praying for them

B. prays that Jesus will heal them and save them

C. ask to be anointed

D. whenever one becomes seriously ill

R︎X _____   **PRESCRIPTION**

True or False   Write **+** if the sentence is true and **O** if it is false.

_+_ **1.** God can bring good out of evil.

_ØT_ **2.** The Sacrament of the Anointing of the Sick can take away sins.

_O_ **3.** The Anointing of the Sick may be received only once.

_O_ **4.** The elderly may be anointed only if they are seriously ill.

_+O_ **5.** The priest anoints the forehead and heart of the sick person with oil.

_ØT_ **6.** The Anointing of the Sick helps a person endure suffering with faith and love.

_+O_ **7.** The Anointing of the Sick can't heal a person's body.

_+_ **8.** It is Jesus who heals and comforts in the Anointing of the Sick.

Germaine Was a Suffering Saint

God's healing love works miracles! Sometimes God works miracles by taking away sickness and suffering. At other times he works an even greater miracle—he gives suffering people the grace to be happy. This is what God did for Germaine, a little girl who lived in France.

Germaine was a true-life Cinderella. She suffered because she was very sickly and had a crippled hand. Besides this, her mother died when Germaine was young. Germaine's stepmother was cruel to her. She made Germaine live in the stable to keep her away from her own children. Germaine's father must not have loved her much either. God did not take Germaine's sufferings away. Instead, he filled her heart with his grace and the joy of his love.

Germaine still loved her parents and helped them by taking care of the sheep. She spun a bundle of wool for her stepmother every day. She loved the villagers too, even though they made fun of her. She told stories about God to younger children, who were not afraid to come to her.

Germaine knew God very well because she often prayed. She prayed the rosary and went to Mass every day. It is said that, before she entered the church, she would plant her staff in the ground and tell the sheep to stay near it. None of them was ever harmed.

Germaine never complained. She shared with the poor the dry bread she was given.

A story is told that one day Germaine took bread she had saved to a sick woman. Her stepmother ran after her. She scolded and beat Germaine until she opened the basket. How surprised the stepmother was to find not bread but flowers! God had worked a miracle for Germaine.

Soon everyone knew that God loved Germaine very much. People started to love and respect her. Even her parents changed. But Germaine did not need their kindness anymore. God took her to heaven when she was only twenty-two.

There, she is no longer sick or crippled. She is a saint who prays for sick and suffering people. More than four hundred people have been cured through her prayers. Others have received the greater miracle of being happy even though they were not cured.

Do you know of someone who has much suffering and yet is happy?

We Remember Germaine

Read these sentences and fill in the missing words.

1. God did not heal Germaine but gave her the grace to be _happy_.

2. Every day Germaine prayed the rosary and went to _mass_.

3. Germaine shared her dry bread with people who were _poor_.

4. Some sick and suffering people who pray to St. Germaine are _heal_.

5. Some people who pray to St. Germaine are not cured but receive the grace to be

happy.

We Pray to St. Germaine

Draw a picture of a sick person you know. Write a prayer to St. Germaine asking her to pray for that person.

Prayer

Dear St. Germaine please help my friend Nick.

A Puzzle on the Sacraments of Healing

Read the clue and choose the correct word from the frame of the puzzle.
Then print the word in the right boxes.

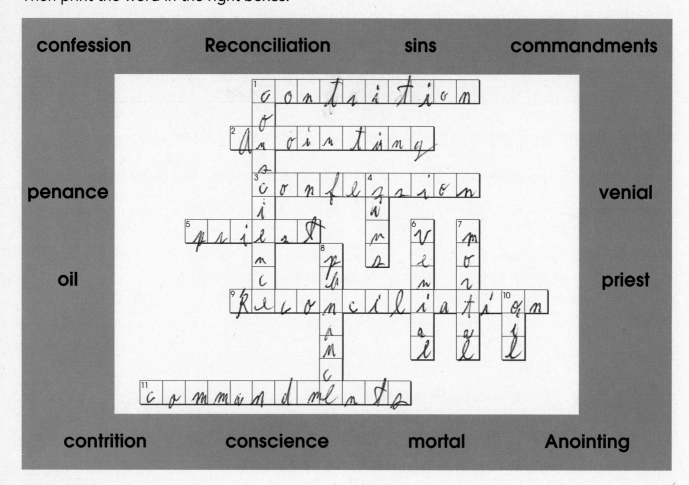

confession   Reconciliation   sins   commandments

penance   venial

oil   priest

contrition   conscience   mortal   Anointing

Across

1. _contrition_ is true sorrow for sin.

2. _Anointing_ of the Sick brings health to the soul and sometimes to the body.

3. _confession_ is the telling of our sins to the priest.

5. A _priest_ should be called for the sick.

9. _Reconciliation_ is a sacrament of God's forgiveness.

11. _commandments_ are God's laws of love.

Down

1. Our _conscience_ helps us to know right and wrong.

4. _Sins_ are failures to love God and others.

6. _Venial_ sins are less serious offenses against God's laws.

7. _Mortal_ sins are serious offenses that separate us from God.

8. _penance_ is prayers or good deeds that make up for our sins.

10. In the Anointing of the Sick the sign of healing is _oil_ .

A Game on Healing Love

Use dice and markers for this game. Throw the dice and move a marker as many spaces as the dice indicate. Write the number on the Scorecard. If you land on a space that names an act of healing love, read the message aloud and add the number given there to your score. The player with the highest score wins.

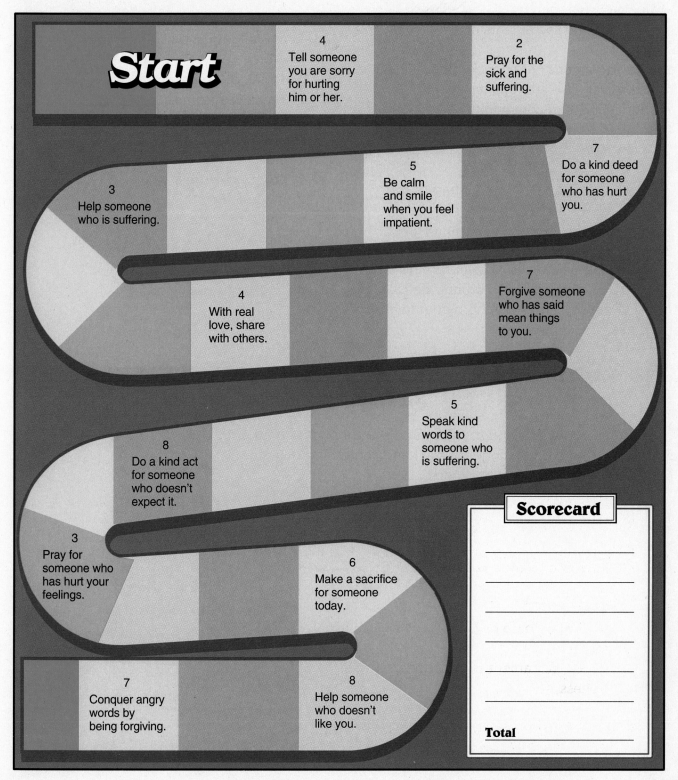

Start

4
Tell someone you are sorry for hurting him or her.

2
Pray for the sick and suffering.

7
Do a kind deed for someone who has hurt you.

3
Help someone who is suffering.

5
Be calm and smile when you feel impatient.

4
With real love, share with others.

7
Forgive someone who has said mean things to you.

5
Speak kind words to someone who is suffering.

8
Do a kind act for someone who doesn't expect it.

3
Pray for someone who has hurt your feelings.

6
Make a sacrifice for someone today.

7
Conquer angry words by being forgiving.

8
Help someone who doesn't like you.

Scorecard

_____

_____

_____

_____

_____

_____

Total

Looking Back at Unit 3

In your study of Unit 3, you have grown in your understanding of God's healing love. You have seen that Jesus continues to heal us through the sacraments of his Church.

In the Sacrament of Reconciliation, our sins are forgiven. We are reconciled with God and the Christian community. We are reminded to make up for our sins and to forgive others as Jesus has forgiven us.

In the Sacrament of the Anointing of the Sick, Jesus continues to show his healing love and to care for the sick. He forgives their sins and sometimes cures their illnesses. Jesus calls us to celebrate his healing love by sharing it with others. He calls us to heal the sick and suffering by our love and prayers.

Living the Message

Can you give yourself a check (✓) for each statement?

❏ 1. I form a right conscience by studying my religion and listening to God's Word.
❏ 2. I think of Jesus' great love to help me stay away from sin.
❏ 3. I celebrate the Sacrament of Reconciliation regularly to receive God's forgiveness and his grace.
❏ 4. I try to change my life and make up for my sins by doing penance.
❏ 5. I help the sick and lonely people through prayer and kind deeds.

Planning to Grow

Let your hand remind you to bring God's healing love to other people. Write on each finger of the hand something you will do to show God's healing love to others.

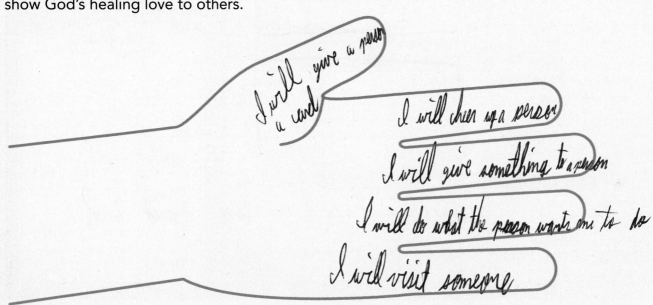

I will give a person a card

I will cheer up a person

I will give something to a person

I will do what the person wants me to do

I will visit someone

FAMILY FEATURE

A Strawberry Reconciliation

Each year the Feke family looks forward to strawberry thanks-giving. This is a Native American celebration that celebrates the early summer moon. It has become a time when people are reconciled to one another. On the day of the celebration the family packs a meal that always includes fresh strawberries, along with shortcake, sugar, and whipped cream. Then they meet with other families for a picnic. Usually someone tells the legend of the origin of the celebration.

A brother and sister went for a walk in the woods. When they came to a fork in the path, the girl wanted to go one way and the boy the other way. After arguing, the girl went her way and the boy went his. As the girl walked down the path, she saw some wonderful things like an old bird's nest and a baby rabbit, but she had no one with whom to share them. If only her brother were with her. Feeling sorry that they had argued, the girl cried, her tears falling onto small bushes. The girl decided to go back and look for her brother. Looking down, she saw to her surprise that on the bushes wherever her tears had fallen, bright red berries appeared. She tried one and discovered it was sweet, so she filled her basket with them and went in search of her brother. When she found him, they ate the berries together. Now when people eat straw-berries they are to forgive and forget.

Your family might celebrate a reconciliation day, preferably before going to celebrate the Sacrament of Reconciliation.

Play soft music and have one of the family members read 1 John 1:5–2:2. Reflect on the reading and then make petitions for faults and sins that might have caused a problem for the family. (Examples: For the times we leave doors unlocked, forgive our thoughtlessness. For being late and keeping others waiting, forgive our thoughtlessness.)

Then have everyone take two pieces of paper. On one the members write something they are sorry for and then crumple it into a ball. On the other they write an intention to improve, folding it to keep as a reminder. The crumpled balls can be burned in a metal pail with sand or dirt on the bottom and a metal lid to cover it, or they can be thrown away as a sign that the family is ready to begin again.

Conclude by reading 1 John 3:18–24.

Then join hands and pray the Our Father and exchange the sign of peace.

Follow this with a strawberry dessert or a whole meal that includes many Native American foods: sandwiches, succotash (corn and lima beans), wild rice, cranberry sauce, and popcorn.

You're the Doctor!

Unscramble the words related to
the sacraments of healing:

1. ANNECEP

_____

2. CEEPA

_____

3. SEFNCSO

_____

4. LIO

_____

5. TTIIOONNCR

_____

6. USBOONATLI

_____

7. CVMITUAI

_____

8. NINONGTIA

_____

Write a prescription for someone's spiritual health:

We Follow Special
Ways to Holiness

UNIT
4

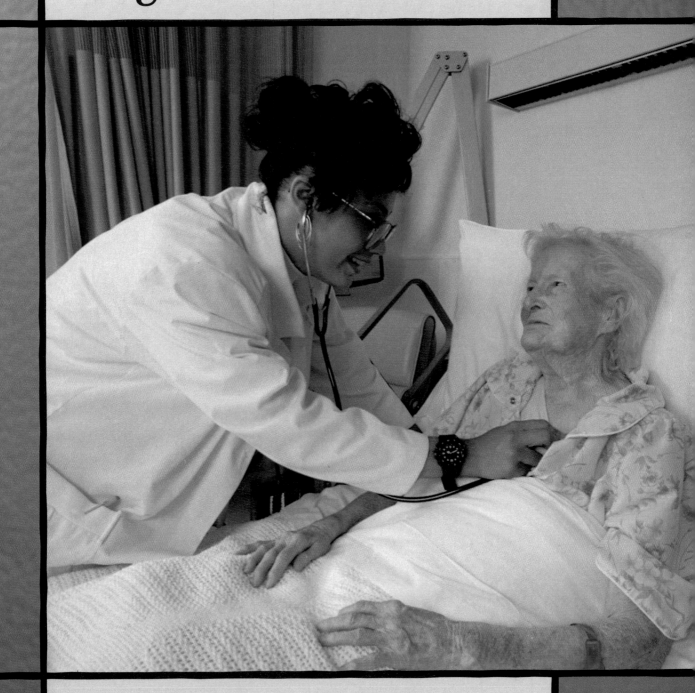

We Follow God's Plan for Our Lives

Have you ever watched a photograph being developed? At first you can barely see the image, but it is there. Slowly it appears brighter and clearer. As it develops, it becomes a perfect image of the subject photographed.

Our lives are somewhat like this picture. God has a special plan for our lives. If we follow this plan, in the end we will have become what God wants us to be. At Baptism, God gave us his life of grace to help us live according to his plan.

All Are Called to Holiness

We are all called to become holy so that we can be happy with God now and forever. That is why God made us. The goal of our lives is to reach holiness. What is holiness? It is sharing God's life and being like God. It is being whole. Holiness is shown in love of God and his people.

Jesus is the holy one. He is perfect in his love for his Father and for all people. To be holy is to be like Jesus. It is to be filled with the Holy Spirit. It is to be a saint!

The Spirit brings . . .

> Love, joy, peace,
> patience,
> kindness, generosity,
> faithfulness, gentleness,
> self-control, *holiness, caringness.*
> Galatians 5:22

In the design below you can discover what God calls all of us to become. Color the triangles to make the message clear.

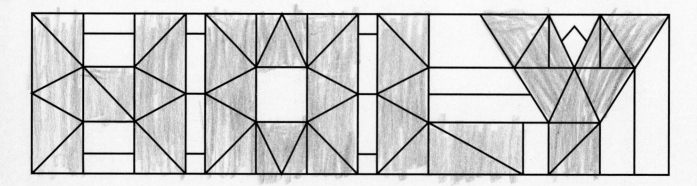

Is holiness an important goal? Yes, it is the most important one of our lives. We may not be able to reach other goals in life, but we should reach this one. It will take a whole lifetime to reach it.

To take part in the Olympic games is a high goal. What does it take to reach such a goal? It takes people who really want to become Olympic stars. They do everything possible to become perfect in a sport. They listen to people who train them. They study how other people became top athletes. They practice and sacrifice for many years. They never give up until they reach their goal.

What does it take to become holy? It takes Christians who really want to be holy. They do everything possible to become perfect in love. With the help of the Holy Spirit, they listen to God's Word and keep it. They try to know Jesus and become like him. They often celebrate the sacraments and take part in the Eucharist. They pray, sacrifice, serve others, and do all that is good. They keep on trying to become holy until God calls them to live in his love forever. Finally, they reach their goal and become saints!

Do you think holy people are happy in this life?

God Gives Special Calls

God's call to holiness is for all his people. But God has a special call for each of us, too. God invites us to become holy by choosing and following a certain way of life. Possible life choices are

- the married life,
- the single life,
- the religious life,
- the permanent diaconate, and
- the priesthood.

The call to a special way of life is a **vocation.** You have studied the sacraments of initiation and the sacraments of healing. Two sacra-

ments give special help to people who follow two very demanding vocations. In this unit you will learn about the two sacraments of vocation: Matrimony and Holy Orders.

We Discover Our Vocations

In order to discover our vocations, we need to pray, asking God to show us which way of life he wants us to follow. God will let us know the way if we open our hearts and listen to the Spirit. God will also give us the courage to do his will for us.

Sometimes God's call comes through other people, such as priests, deacons, brothers, sisters, parents, or friends. They may inspire us to follow their way of life. We may talk to them about their vocations and ask them to help us know ours. We may also hear God's call through the things that happen in our lives. Maybe God will simply put a great desire in our hearts for one special vocation. God calls in many different ways. We will hear God's call if we remember that he is with us and if we do his will.

We Prepare for Our Vocations

We can do things now that will help us to get ready for our special vocations. We can be alert to the needs of others and help them. We can be responsible in doing our duties. We can be truthful, honest, pure, and obedient. We can learn what our talents are and develop them as best we can. We can pray and celebrate the sacraments.

Planning Ahead

In the spaces below write or draw pictures of things you can do to prepare for your vocation.

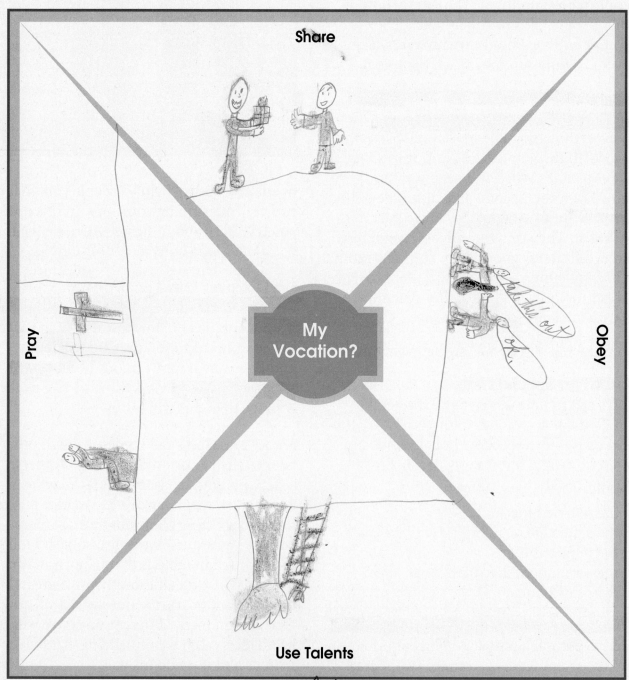

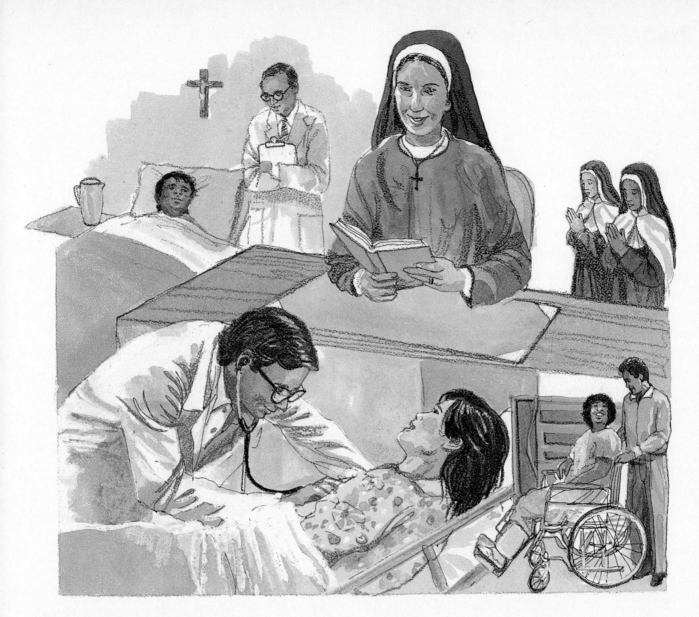

The Religious Vocation

God chooses some people to enter into a special covenant of love with him. Brother and sister religious and priests who belong to a religious order are called to love and serve God and God's people in a unique way. Jesus promised them joy in this life and happiness with him forever. He told us:

 "Everyone who has given up houses or brothers or sisters or father or mother or children or lands for the sake of my name will receive a hundred times more, and will inherit eternal life."

Matthew 19:29

Religious make public promises to God called **vows.** In these vows they give themselves to God and the service of his people. Vows are a love gift to the Lord. Religious pray much and celebrate the sacraments often. They are helped by the other members of their communities. Together they pray, work, eat, and enjoy good times. They share their joys and sorrows as well as their love for God and others. To show they belong to a certain community, some religious wear special clothing, called a habit, or an emblem or pin and a ring.

Religious are special witnesses to Christ's love. Their life of prayer reminds us of God's presence and brings us God's blessings. They help us to know God's goodness and love. Their works show Jesus serving people in our world today.

r = our job

The ministries, or apostolic services, of men and women religious vary. Some religious devote their lives mainly to prayer but spend a few hours each day serving God in manual labor. They may be carpenters, farmers, or cooks. They may make altar bread and vestments. Other religious bring God's Good News to people by teaching, doing parish work, or promoting peace and justice. Some bring God's healing love and care to the sick, the poor, the suffering, orphans, the handicapped, and the elderly. Religious who are ordained witness to Jesus by giving priestly service to the Church. In many ways religious live the Gospel message and build up God's kingdom.

The Single Vocation

More and more Christians are being called to be holy as single people. Some people choose to be unmarried all their lives. Married people also were single before they married and become single when they separate or divorce or when their partners die. Single people do not have many of the responsibilities of marriage or religious life. They are freer to develop their interests and talents and able to deepen their spiritual life and minister to others. Single people are often the backbone of communities. With their gifts they support activities and programs that lead people to God and care for others' needs. They witness Christ to all those with whom they are involved in the world. Single people find joy in loving and serving others.

My Vocation Prayer

Dear Jesus, you followed your Father's plan when you lived on earth. Help me to know my vocation and to follow it. Give the Church good Christian families and laypersons. May they love and serve you. Send holy bishops, priests, and deacons to give us the sacraments. Send good sisters and brothers to pray and work for your kingdom.

Lord Jesus send more workers to spred your kingdom.

St. Elizabeth Ann Seton Had Three Vocations

Growing up in New York just after the Revolutionary War, Elizabeth Bayley could not have guessed the great things God had planned for her. Elizabeth was called by God to the married life. Everyone could see how Elizabeth and William Seton loved each other. On her wedding day Elizabeth prayed, "Dear God, thank you for William."

God blessed Elizabeth and her husband with five children. Their family was happy during those first years. Then one day William came home very worried. He explained that his shipping business was not good. There would be very little money for their family. Elizabeth felt more sorry for William than for herself.

Soon afterward William became very ill, and the doctor told him to go to Italy for a rest. William's friends, the Filicchis, lived there. He could rest in their home and get well. Elizabeth and their oldest daughter, Anna Marie, went to Italy with William. The other children had to be left with relatives, although Elizabeth was sorry to do this. In Italy, William's health did not improve. Elizabeth prayed and helped her husband all she could, but he died in his wife's arms shortly after they arrived.

The Filicchis were very kind to Elizabeth. They let her stay with them for about a year. They were Catholics who really lived their faith. Elizabeth came to know Jesus in these people who were so much like him. She prayed and went to Mass with them every day.

On her way back to New York, Elizabeth decided to become a Catholic. This was a hard decision for her to make because she knew her family would disown her. A priest taught Elizabeth about the Catholic faith. She and her children were baptized.

After that Elizabeth's relatives and friends would not speak to her or help her. Still, Elizabeth trusted in God. She started to teach in a small school near her home and did well for a while. Then the people began to complain that Elizabeth was a Catholic. They took their children out of school, and she met hard times again.

Just at this time, a priest in Baltimore invited Elizabeth to come and start a Catholic school there. Bishop Carroll also sent for her. He wrote: "Come to us, Mrs. Seton. You have a lot of courage. We need you for God's work." So Elizabeth and her family went to Baltimore.

Before long, women and young girls were writing to Elizabeth, asking whether they could help her. Then Elizabeth realized that God was calling her to give her life to him as a religious. She and the other women who helped her began a religious community. They became known as the Daughters of Charity. Today many Daughters of Charity carry on Mother Seton's work.

Is Dr. Tom Dooley a Saint?

"If you are a saint, your halo is mighty crooked!" joked one of Tom Dooley's friends. Tom laughed with his friend. He knew that he was far from being a saint.

Today many people think that Tom Dooley really was a saint. A saint is a person who reaches the goal of holiness. Anyone who knew Tom Dooley knew that he never went halfway to reach any goal; he went the whole way. When he studied French as a boy in St. Louis, he learned it well. When he collected for the poor and the missions, he went to every person he could. When he wanted to become a doctor, he studied hard at the University of Notre Dame. Then he went on to medical school. In 1953 Tom started his life's work as a Navy doctor. His first orders were to care for suffering refugees in Vietnam. He loved these Asian people. He admired their love and respect for children and elderly people.

When Tom saw the sufferings of these people, his whole life was changed. He decided to give up his dream of becoming a great Navy surgeon. Instead, he devoted his life to the people in Southeast Asia.

"Why do you want to make so great a sacrifice?" asked one of Tom's friends. Tom's answer came right from his heart. "I just want to do what I can for people who don't have it so good."

One of Tom's projects was called Operation Laos. In Laos he set up clinics and hospitals for the sick. This project needed more than what one person could do. Before long, some doctors saw what Tom was doing. They went to Laos to work with him. To them Tom explained, "Our work here has meaning when we remember Christ's words, 'What you do to my people, you do to me.'"

Tom's project also needed money and supplies. To raise money, Tom wrote books and went on speaking tours. In this way he was able to ship medicine, food, and medical equipment to Laos.

Tom spent long hours teaching the Asian people to take care of their own sick people. How these people loved their American doctor! They would bow low when they met him. Tom never liked this and would say, "Don't worship me or anyone else—worship God!"

In 1961 Dr. Dooley came back to New York for the last time. He was dying of cancer and went to the hospital. When a priest friend visited him, Tom was suffering much pain but was in good spirits. His words tell us how this could be. Tom said, "If this is the way God wants it to be, this is the way I want it, too." Tom Dooley died on January 19, 1961. He had reached his greatest goal. In thirty-four years, he had done what few others have done in many years of life.

Father John Paul and lives in a rectory.

Things to Do at Home

1. Plant some flower seeds. Watch them grow into beautiful flowers. Compare them to your life. Are you doing what you can to become what God wants you to be? Will you bear fruit (the fruit of good works) for him? Will you become "something beautiful for God"?
2. Discuss with your mother or father how you are preparing for your vocation.
3. Pray a Hail Mary in your night prayers. Ask Mary to guide you to do with your life what God wants you to do.
4. Talk to two people who have different vocations. Ask them what they like about their vocations. Ask what advice they would give someone who wants to follow those vocations.

We Remember

What does God call everyone to be? *Study*
God calls everyone to be holy.

What is a vocation? *Study*
A vocation is a call from God to follow a special way of life.

Words to Know
vocation
priest, brother and sister religious
vows

We Respond

Lord, help me prepare now for my

vocation by _____

_____

_____

_____

We Review

Getting Ready List five ways to prepare for your vocation:

1. *I can help others.*
2. *I can pray.*
3. *I can celebrate the sacraments.*
4. *I can study.*
5. *I so should be obedi obey people*

Sister Barbra is in the Holy family of nazareth

Living Happily Read each sentence and choose the correct word from the box to fill in the blank lines.

| love | community | know | Christians | vocation | serve | religious |

1. All *Christians* are called to holiness.

2. God has a special *vocation* for each of us.

3. We pray to *know* God's will and to have the courage to do it.

4. Priest, sisters, and brothers who make vows are called *religious*.

5. Religious usually live in a *community*

6. Religious love God and *serve* the Church.

7. Single people can bring Jesus' *love* to others.

Marriage Is a Sacrament of Faithful Love

Everyone loves a good story! One of the most wonderful stories is how your mom and dad decided to get married. This story is very important because it tells you about the beginnings of your family.

Every family's story is meant to be one of love. When family members really love one another, they are willing to sacrifice for one another. When family members work to bring happiness to one another, they do as God himself does. Then each person grows in happiness and holiness.

Jesus' special family, the Church, began with love. Jesus loved us so much that he willingly gave his life for us. Through his death he gave life to his Church. Jesus helps us who are baptized to grow in his life and love. He wants every member of his Church to be happy with him forever.

The Sacrament of Marriage, or Matrimony, is a sign of Jesus' love for his Church and his union with it. When a man and a woman love each other very much and want to give themselves to each other, they may celebrate this sacrament. They live together as a new family. Before they marry, they must decide to help each other make their love grow. Their love reminds people of Jesus' great love for his Church.

The Marriage Ceremony Unites a Couple For Life

Catholics usually choose to be married during Mass. They ask Jesus to strengthen them to keep the covenant that they make with each other.

The marriage ceremony begins after the Liturgy of the Word. The priest's words remind the bride and groom of God's wonderful love for them. He tells them that God will bless and strengthen them.

In the presence of God, a priest, and the Christian community the bride and groom make this promise to each other:

I promise to be true to you in good times and in bad, in sickness and in health. I will love and honor you all the days of my life.

Rite of Marriage

They confer, or minister, the sacrament on each other. This exchange of promises, or **marriage vows,** is the sign in the Sacrament of Marriage. Through it Christ unites a man and a woman as husband and wife for their entire lives.

The husband and wife may place a ring on each other's finger. It reminds them to be faithful in love.

After the Lord's Prayer in the Mass, the priest gives the bride and groom a special blessing, called a **nuptial blessing.** In it he asks God the Father to bless the couple and to give them the graces they need. He also

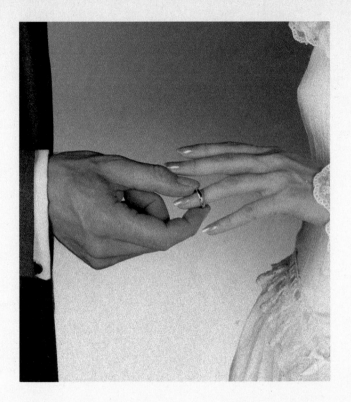

asks God's blessing to make them good parents. These blessings last all through their lives.

Find out the story of a couple's marriage. Fill in the information below.

_My mom and dad_____ celebrate the anniversary of their marriage each year on _Mar 3_.

They were married on that date in 19_89_ at

_____ Church in _____.

The members of their family are

_____.

Unselfish Love Strengthens a Marriage

In marriage <u>a man and a woman try to make their love grow.</u> It is not always easy. They must live their lives together even when it is difficult. They have to try hard to solve their problems.

How can people grow in love when they disagree about many things? They should

- put each other first.
- try to make each other happy.
- learn to talk to each other about their problems and solve them in a way that is not too hard for either of them. *communicate*
- learn to ask and give forgiveness when one has hurt the other.
- <u>spend some time each day praying together, asking the Holy Spirit's help.</u>

Someday God may call you to become holy in marriage. Will you be ready to do whatever God asks with unselfish love?

Joe and Sheila are twins. They often disagree but both try to be unselfish. How can they practice unselfish love in the following situations?

Sheila wants all the children in the family to put their money together to buy their mother and father each a nice birthday gift. Joe wants each child to buy a gift with his or her own money.

They can get one big one

Sheila likes to watch science-fiction programs on television. Joe likes to watch sports shows.

They can take turns.

On Friday evening the family gets supper from a fast-food place. Sheila always wants pizza. Joe always wants to go to a hamburger place.

They can take turns.

Marriage Lasts

Marriage is a sacrament that lasts for a lifetime. It is not over when the wedding clothes are changed. The grace of this sacrament remains with a husband and wife all of their lives.

This grace will help both partners make each other happy. It will help them to grow in love for God and each other. It will help each to become holy.

Sometimes married couples have hard times. Maybe one of them loses a job. Then there is not enough money to live as they would like. The grace of marriage will help the husband and wife. It will help them find ways to spend less money and to be happy with fewer things. It will give them strength to find a job.

It might happen that the husband or wife is hurt or becomes sick. The other person will have more work to do, but God will give the grace that is needed. The person who is sick or hurt will find it hard to watch the other

do all the work. God will help both of them. If they accept God's grace, they will have peace in their hearts.

Children Are Living Reminders of Love

Children are the greatest natural gift God gives to married couples. He uses the love of the husband and the wife to give life to a child. The child should be a reminder to the parents of their love for each other and God's love for them both. Together they surround the children of their family with love. Their love shows the children God's love. They teach them to love God as their Father. Children who are loved will learn to love others too. The grace of the Sacrament of Marriage helps the husband and wife to be good parents.

Sometimes—because of death, separation or divorce, or other causes—a family is left with just one parent. God still loves this family very much. He helps that parent take care of the family.

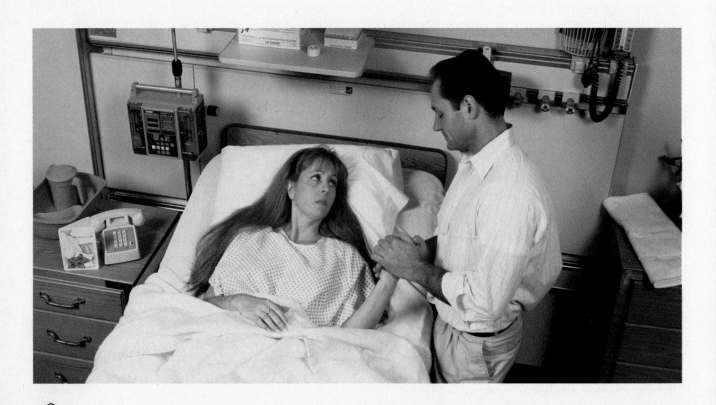

Children can bring blessings to their parents. Even as babies they bring much joy to the family. No two children are alike. Each child is special in his or her own way. Members of a family can bring deep joy or deep sorrow to one another. The pain of one member of the family also hurts the others. The joy of one member brings joy to all.

Parents are willing to sacrifice many things in order to take care of their children. They are happy to do this because they love their children.

Think of some ways children can show gratitude to their parents. Write them.

Do what they say

———————————————

———————————————

Children can show their love and gratitude as they grow up. They can do this in a special way when their parents are older. Children should also have a special love for their grandparents.

Write some ways boys and girls your age can show love for their grandparents.

I can show love by supporting them.

———————————————

Each person must know that he or she is loved by the family. Some boys and girls are the only children in their families. Others have brothers or sisters. God works differently in each family. The important thing is that every member be loved. We can tell people we love them, but we should also show our love by the way we act. Even just

I pray for your parents

listening to others when they talk to us shows our love.

Think of some ways a child your age can show brothers and sisters that they are loved. Write them.

I can give them complement

———————————————

A family is a group of people of different ages. They are related through marriage and should love one another. They should help one another grow more loving as they serve God and one another. They should also share their love with others and help bring Christ to the world.

Are you helping to make your family the family God wants it to be?

Things to Do at Home

1. Ask your parents or another couple to tell you about their wedding day. If they have a photo album, look at it with them.
2. Invite your parents to help you look through the newspapers. Find articles that tell about marriage or family life. Decide whether the articles talk about marriage or family life according to the teachings of Christ. Be ready to share your findings with the class.
3. Plan a special way to show your love for the other members of your family. It might be a simple note under each plate at supper saying, "Thank you for being you!"
4. Write a prayer for your family.

We Remember

What does the Sacrament of Marriage do?
The Sacrament of Marriage joins a man and woman together for their entire lives. It helps them to love one another faithfully, to grow in holiness, and to love and educate the children God sends to them.

Words to Know
Matrimony
marriage vow
nuptial blessing

We Respond

Father, by following the example of the holy family of your Son in mutual love and respect, may we come to the joy of our home in heaven.
> from the *Opening Prayer of the Mass for the Family*

We Review

Virtues for Marriage   Name three virtues or qualities that would help people to be happily married.

Show mutual love
joy
and respect

Love and Marriage   Fill in the missing words using the list in the two hearts.

parents
grace
Church

ring
gratitude
nuptial
vows

1. The Sacrament of Marriage is a sign of Jesus' love for his ___*Church*___ .

2. The bride and groom confer the Sacrament of Marriage on each other when they say their ___*vows*___ .

3. A ___*ring*___ is a visible sign of their promises to be faithful forever.

4. During the marriage the priest gives the bride and groom a special ___*nuptial*___ blessing.

5. The ___*grace*___ of the Sacrament of Marriage helps a man and woman keep their vows and become holy.

6. The grace of the Sacrament of Marriage helps the husband and wife to be good ___*parent*___ .

7. Children owe their parents love and ___*gratitude*___ .

Priests Are Christ's Ordained Ministers

Deacon Jim knelt before the bishop. In silence the bishop placed both his hands on Jim's head. He did the same for all of the deacons who had been Jim's classmates. This action showed that the bishop was sharing the priesthood of Christ with the man before him. Then, one by one, each of the other priests placed his hands on the men's heads, showing that they all share in the priesthood.

After that the candidates placed themselves in a semicircle before the bishop. As the bishop extended his hands over them, he began a prayer of consecration. Jim listened carefully to the words. He heard the bishop say:

> Almighty Father,
> grant to these servants of yours
> the dignity of the priesthood.

Jim was now a priest! Through the laying on of the bishop's hands and the prayer of consecration he was ordained a priest. All the years of prayer, study, and parish work had led up to this moment.

An assisting priest placed a **stole,** a long, narrow vestment that is a sign of the priesthood, around Father Jim's neck and over both shoulders. He then gave Father a **chasuble,** a large, full vestment like a cloak, worn over the other vestments at Mass.

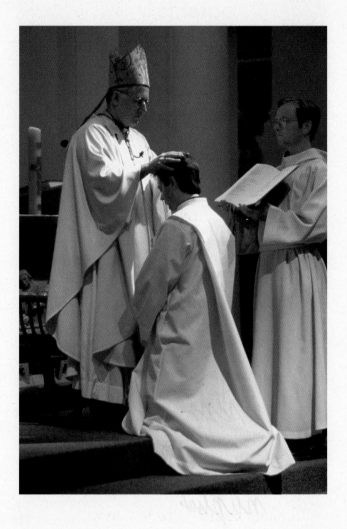

Other priests did the same for each of the newly ordained priests.

Then the bishop anointed Father Jim's palms with holy **chrism.** Jesus used his hands to bless children and to cure the sick. He used them to change bread and wine into his Body and Blood and to offer himself to his Father. The priest acts in

Christ's place. He uses his hands in the same way. The bishop prayed:

> The Father anointed our Lord Jesus Christ
> through the power of the Holy Spirit.
> May Jesus preserve you to sanctify the Christian people
> and to offer sacrifice to God.
> *Rite of the Ordination of a Priest*

Then the bishop gave Father Jim and the other newly ordained priests each a paten and a chalice. The paten had bread on it. The chalice contained water and wine. This action is a sign that priests have the ministry of presiding at the Eucharist.

The newly ordained priests then joined with the bishop in celebrating the Mass. They prayed the Eucharistic Prayer with him. Together they consecrated the bread and wine. When priests celebrate Mass together, it is called **concelebration.** The newly ordained also joined the bishop for the final blessing.

We Share Christ's Priesthood
At Baptism we received a share in Christ's priesthood. As Catholic Christians we are called to join with Christ in the offering of himself to the Father. We are called to worship, praise, petition, and thank God as Jesus did. Confirmation strengthens our union with Jesus. It gives us a greater share in his priesthood. This priesthood we all share is called the **common priesthood.**

Holy Orders gives a Christian another kind of sharing in Christ's priesthood. The priest is called by the Church and marked forever to act in the person of Christ. He proclaims the Word of God and celebrates the Eucharist.

He forgives sin and heals the sick. He receives new members into the Church. He prays the Liturgy of the Hours in the name of the Church. He belongs to the **ordained priesthood.** The rite of the Sacrament of Holy Orders is called **ordination.**

Christ's plan is to live and work in the world today. While he was still on earth, he sent the apostles to continue his work among the people. They, in turn, passed on this mission to the bishops, priests, and deacons who came after them. We should pray each day for bishops, priests, and deacons. They need strength to carry on the work of Jesus with love.

A Prayer for Priests
Lord Jesus, bless all our priests. Help them to realize that through their sacred calling they act for you in a special way. Give them a great spirit of love and generosity that they may be true to you all the days of their priestly life. May all they bless and do in your name be holy. Amen.

Priestly Life Is a Mission of Service

Through the Sacrament of Holy Orders, Father Jim has dedicated his life to the service of God's people. He now works to bring others closer to God. He works with and for the Christian community.

The pictures on this page show the three main works of a priest. Find their titles on the next page. Print each on the line beneath the picture it matches.

_____

_____

_____

Proclaiming God's Word

Father Jim was excited about going to Holy Spirit Parish. He thought about one of his main duties as a priest. In St. Mark's Gospel he read that Jesus told his apostles,

"Go into the whole world and proclaim the gospel to every creature."

Mark 16:15

Father realized that proclaiming the Good News is one of his most important works. He will not only read it to others but he will explain it to them. He will help them see how God speaks to them in his written word and in the Church.

Celebrating the Sacraments

Father Jim will perform many other sacred works. Celebrating the Eucharist with God's people will be Father's greatest privilege. It will be the source of all his energy and love. It will bring people closer to Christ. In Baptism he will receive new members into the family of Jesus. He will speak Jesus' words of peace and forgiveness in the Sacrament of Reconciliation. To the sick and dying, Father will bring Jesus' healing in the Anointing of the Sick. He will witness and bless the bride and groom in the Sacrament of Marriage.

Strengthening the Community

Father Jim will build up the Christian community at Holy Spirit Parish. He will plan activities that help the people love God and one another more. When Christians gather together, they show that they are one with Christ.

Priestly Ministries Vary

Some priests are religious and belong to communities such as the Benedictines, Jesuits, Dominicans, and Franciscans. Some are missionaries at home or in foreign lands. Not all priests serve in parishes. Some are chaplains in hospitals or colleges, teachers, or counselors. Others work in diocesan offices or devote their lives to prayer.

Name a priest who has an unusual ministry.

_____

What does he do?

_____

Through the Sacrament of Holy Orders, Jesus continues his work on earth today. We should pray that more people will answer God's call and serve God's people as priests.

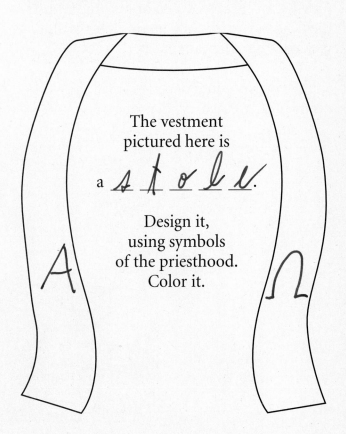

The vestment pictured here is a _stole_.

Design it, using symbols of the priesthood. Color it.

Deacons Are Ordained to Serve

1 Deacons share in the Sacrament of Holy Orders. They are ordained by the bishop to serve in the Church. They help the bishops and priests continue the work of Christ. There are two kinds of deacons.

Some deacons are preparing for the priesthood. After completing their studies they are ordained priests. In that way they share more fully in the Sacrament of Holy Orders.

2 Married or unmarried men who are at least thirty-five years old may be ordained as **permanent deacons.** They serve God and the Church in a special way. These men have a three-to-five-year training period. During this time they study and help in the parishes.

The bishop ordains someone a deacon by laying his hands on the man's head and praying for him. As a sign of his ordination, the deacon wears a stole on his left shoulder. It crosses his chest and back.

What a deacon does depends upon the needs of the parish. All deacons show love for God and his people. They work for the Church in the name of Jesus.

Deacons may serve in the ways listed here. Check what you have seen a deacon do.

- ❏ assist in the liturgy
- ❏ preside at Baptism
- ❏ distribute Holy Communion
- ❏ read the Scriptures and preach a homily
- ❏ teach in the parish school or other religious education programs
- ❏ lead Bible and prayer services
- ❏ perform charitable works for the poor, the sick, the elderly, and others in need
- ❏ guide people in their works of mercy and in their efforts to become holy
- ❏ preside at weddings

We can pray for deacons as the bishop did at their ordination:

Lord, send forth upon them the Holy Spirit to strengthen them to carry out faithfully the work of the ministry.

adapted from the
Rite of the Ordination of Deacons

Getting to Know a Deacon

What deacon serves in your parish or nearby?

_____

To learn more about him and his work, what questions could you ask?

_____

Bishops Have the Fullness of Priesthood

Some priests are called to the fullness of priesthood by being appointed bishops by the pope. A bishop ordains them through the laying on of hands, anointing with chrism, and a prayer. Bishops are successors of the apostles and the chief shepherds of the Church. They teach and lead us in the place of Jesus. They help us to be holy people of God. The symbols of their special ministry are a ring, a **miter** (a tall, pointed hat), and a **crosier** (a staff). Most bishops lead and care for people within a certain area called a **diocese.** The pope is the bishop of Rome.

We Remember

What is Holy Orders?

Holy Orders is the sacrament that makes a man an ordained bishop, priest, or deacon. He can then act for Christ in a special way.

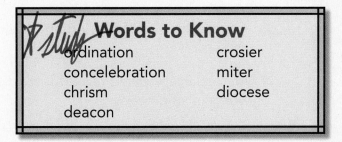

Words to Know

ordination   crosier
concelebration   miter
chrism   diocese
deacon

Things to Do at Home

1. Share with your family what you have learned about the priesthood as a mission of service. Invite family members to tell how a priest has been of service to them. Say together the prayer for priests on page 129.
2. Send a "Thank-you-gram" to your parish priest. Thank him for all he has done for the parish, for your family, and for you.
3. Find out about the different ministries of priests in your diocese.
4. Make a booklet of famous bishops or a booklet about your diocesan bishop.

We Respond

Mary, Queen of the Clergy, pray for bishops, priests, and deacons.

We Review

Priestly Ordination   Choose the matching term and place its letter on the line.

_____ **1.** The only person who is able to ordain

_____ **2.** Long, narrow vestment that is a sign of the priesthood

_____ **3.** To bring someone into the order of priesthood

_____ **4.** Oil used to anoint the priest's hands at his ordination

_____ **5.** Christ's priesthood as shared by all baptized persons

_____ **6.** Full vestment worn over all the other vestments at Mass

_____ **7.** A celebration of the Sacrament of Holy Orders

_____ **8.** Christ's priesthood as shared by a person who receives the Sacrament of Holy Orders

A. ordination
B. common priesthood
C. chasuble
D. bishop
E. ordain
F. ordained priesthood
G. stole
H. chrism
I. priest

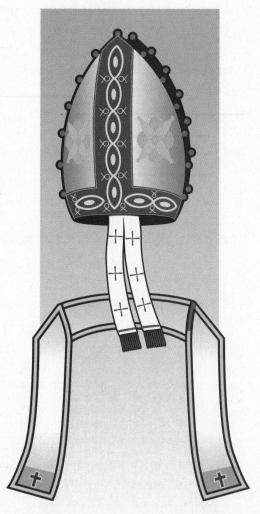

Servants of the Church   Identify the person(s) described. Write the letter(s) on the line.

   A. priests   **B.** deacons   **C.** bishops

_____ **1.** Are appointed by the pope

_____ **2.** Are ordained by the laying on of hands and a prayer

_____ **3.** Are especially called to perform charitable works for the needy

_____ **4.** Wear a stole over the left shoulder

_____ **5.** Usually teach and lead a diocese

_____ **6.** May preside at a wedding

_____ **7.** Can consecrate bread and wine at the Eucharist

_____ **8.** Have a crosier and a miter

Listening to His Call

On the blanks below, print the letter of the alphabet that comes before each letter that is shown. Then you will find a message from Scripture on how to follow your call to be holy.

Let Us Do Good To All.

M F U   V T   E P   H P P E   U P   B M M

Galatians 6:10

Read the question and find the answer in the New Testament. Write the answer on the lines below.

1. What did Jesus tell Peter and Andrew when he called them?   Matthew 4:18–20

Jesus said, "Come after me, and I will make you fishers of men

2. What did Mary answer when God called her?   Luke 1:26–38

Mary said, "Behold, I am the handmaid of the Lord.

3. What did Mary tell us to do when Jesus speaks to us?   John 2:1–5

Do whatever he tells you.

Vocations

Write a particular way each of these people becomes holy in his or her vocation. The first one is done for you.

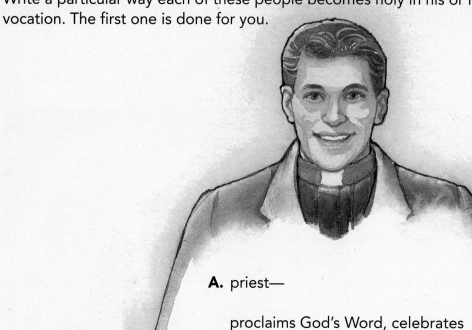

A. priest—

proclaims God's Word, celebrates the sacraments, and strengthens the Christian community

B. single person—

A single person can donate money to the missions and witness Christ at work. They can also deepen spiritual life

C. man or woman religious—

can preach to the people who don't know Christ.

D. married person—

can share their love with each other

E. deacon—

can baptism a person and bring a new person into the church.

F. bishop—

can confirm a person in the sacrament of Confirmation.

Make a Path to the Lord

The choices we make each day prepare us to follow our vocations. Wise choices help us on our way to Jesus.

Read the signs in order, starting with sign #1. Draw a line connecting only those signs that tell something you should do to prepare for your vocation.

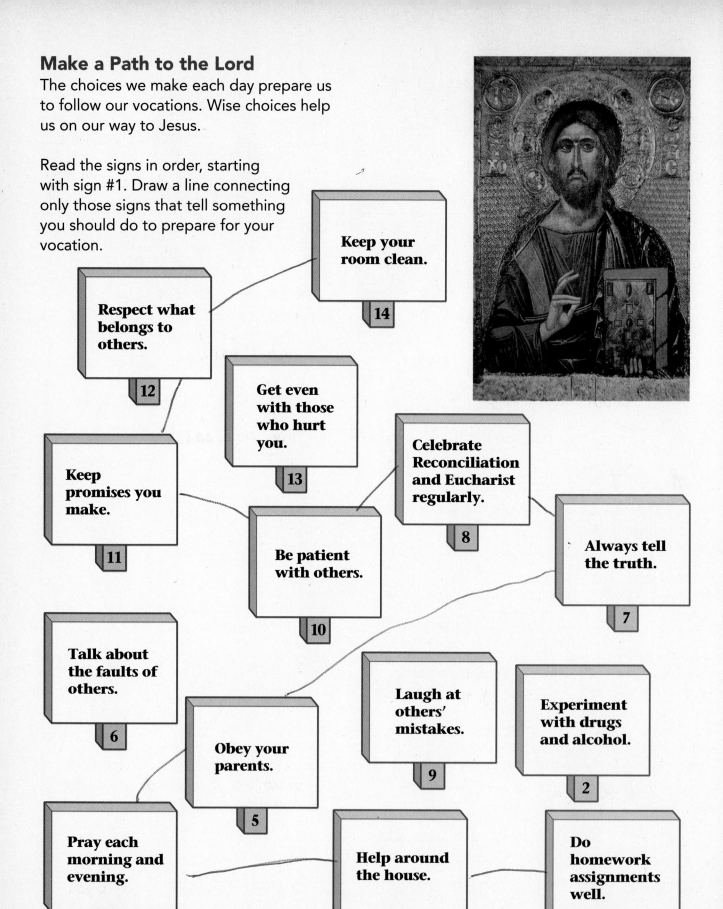

Keep your room clean.
14

Respect what belongs to others.
12

Get even with those who hurt you.
13

Celebrate Reconciliation and Eucharist regularly.
8

Keep promises you make.
11

Be patient with others.
10

Always tell the truth.
7

Talk about the faults of others.
6

Obey your parents.
5

Laugh at others' mistakes.
9

Experiment with drugs and alcohol.
2

Pray each morning and evening.
4

Help around the house.
3

Do homework assignments well.
1

The Seven Sacraments

In column 2 write the sacrament's name and what Jesus does for us in it.

Sacrament	What Jesus Does for Us	Signs of What Jesus Does
	Cleanses from sin; makes us children of God; makes us members of the Church	Water "I baptize you in the name of the Father, and of the Son, and of the Holy Spirit."
	Confirmation / strengthens our faith; unites us more closely to the Church; commits us more to Christ; makes us strong witnesses	Chrism (oil) with the laying on of the hand "[Name], be sealed with the Gift of the Holy Spirit."
	Holy Eucharist / nourishes and strengthens; unites us with Jesus and one another.	Bread and wine "This is my body. . . . This is my blood."
	Reconciliation / heals us; forgives our sins; brings us into closer union with God and one another.	Sins told with sorrow "I absolve you from your sins, in the name of the Father, and of the Son, and of the Holy Spirit."
	Marriage / joins a man and woman for life; helps them love one another faithfully; grow in holiness; love and teach the children given into them.	"I, [Name], take you, [Name], to be my _____. I promise to be true to you in good times and in bad, in sickness and in health. I will love you and honor you all the days of my life."
	Holy Orders / makes a man an ordained bishop, priest, or deacon; helps him act in a special way of service to the church	The laying on of hands "Almighty Father, grant to these servants of yours the dignity of the priesthood."
	Anointing of the sick / brings health to the soul and sometimes to the body; comforts and strengthens the sick.	Oil of the sick "Through this holy anointing may the Lord in his love and mercy help you with the grace of the Holy Spirit. May the Lord who frees you from sin save you and raise you up."

Looking Back at Unit 4

In your study of Unit 4 you have become more aware of God's love for us. He calls us to holiness and to serve the Church.

You have learned about vocations. Some people are called to serve the Church as bishops, priests, or deacons. Some are called to married life, single life, or religious life. In all these vocations God gives his people the grace to become holy.

Religious promise to love God in a special way of life. They try to live the Gospel message more fully and build up God's kingdom. Single people lead lives of dedicated service.

Through the Sacrament of Marriage, God blesses a man and a woman, helps them to be faithful to each other, and blesses them with children. He gives them grace to teach their children to know and love him.

Through the Sacrament of Holy Orders, Christ continues his priestly work. Men receive powers to bring Christ to his people as bishops, priests, and deacons.

You have learned to pray that the Holy Spirit will guide us to do God's will.

Living the Message

Can you give yourself a check (✓) for each statement?

❏ **1.** I thank God for the grace of my Baptism.
☑ **2.** I try each day to grow in holiness.
☑ **3.** I am preparing now for my vocation.
❏ **4.** I pray for good deacons, priests, bishops, and religious.
☑ **5.** I pray for good families and loving single people in God's Church.

Planning to Grow

On the lines by the flowers, write five things you can do to prepare for your vocation. Color the flowers as a sign of your growth.

study

read a book

Do kind acts

don't say mean words

share

FAMILY FEATURE

Easter Eggs

For generations the Welych family have passed on the custom of decorating Easter eggs with wax and dye. Weeks before Easter, Mrs. Welych begins. She takes the metal lid from a coffee can and places a piece of pure beeswax on it over a low flame. Then she sticks a straight pin into the flat end of a long wooden matchstick. When the wax is melted, she dips the head of the pin into the wax and quickly makes strokes on a hard-boiled egg to create beautiful designs. When she and the Welych children dip these eggs into brilliant egg dye, the eggs turn into lovely symbols of Christ's new life. When the eggs are dry, a coat of varnish is applied to seal the patterns.

The Welych family places some of the decorated eggs in a basket with other Easter food to be blessed at their parish church on Holy Saturday morning.

The egg itself stands for Christ's tomb. Just as a chick emerges from the shell, Christ came out of the tomb with new life. The custom of exchanging eggs at Easter began in the Middle Ages when during Lent people did not eat eggs.

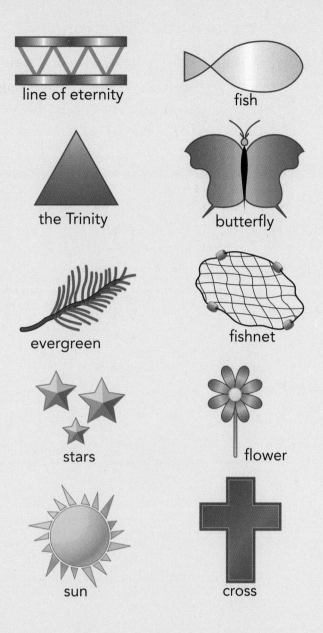

line of eternity

fish

the Trinity

butterfly

evergreen

fishnet

stars

flower

sun

cross

Your family might wish to decorate eggs with wax and give them to your friends and relatives. Instead of using beeswax, you may prefer just to draw designs on the eggs with crayons. Above are some simplified designs based on traditional symbols that Eastern Europeans use on their Easter eggs.

Virtues for Vocations

For any vocation certain qualities are needed and should be developed. For each letter in the mirror write a good quality that begins with that letter.

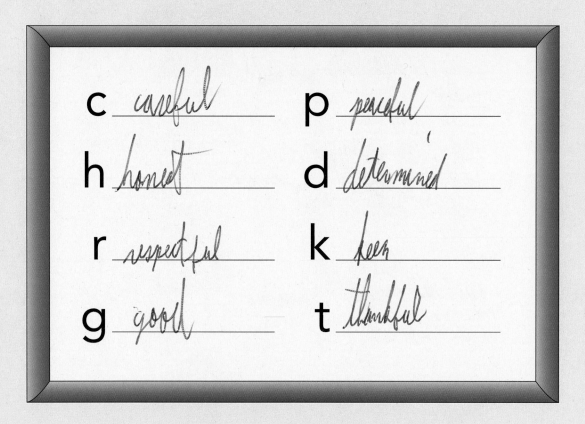

c _careful_   p _peaceful_

h _honest_   d _determined_

r _respectful_   k _keen_

g _good_   t _thankful_

Choose a vocation and tell how some of the qualities above will be needed to carry it out well.

Vocation

_____

_____

_____

We Worship God by Living in Love

Life Is a Gift from God

Betty Jane gets excited every spring as she helps her mother plant the family garden. This year they planted flowers and vegetables. It was hard to believe that those hard little seeds held life! A few days after planting, however, there were tiny green shoots peeping through the earth. Betty liked to get up early and run outside to look at her garden. She had seen it many times, but it still was a miracle to her. In her mind she saw ripe vegetables and beautiful flowers. She thought about how wonderful and kind God is to give life. She knew this garden was God's gift to her.

One day she was shocked to find that someone had pulled out all the little plants. They all looked dead! Betty Jane was crying when her mother came outside. They took each wilted plant, replanted it, and gave it water. Some plants were really dead. A few looked as though they would perk up with loving care. Betty Jane and her mother talked about how to care for the plants. She still worried: "What if someone pulled them out again? Would they live?"

Someone had not shown respect for Betty Jane's garden or for Betty Jane. In killing her plants, the person had hurt her.

All Life Is in Our Care

All life comes from God. He created all things and gave some of them the gift of life. When God created people, he gave them the special gift of human life. God also created them in his own image and gave them a life that will last forever. God looked at all he had created. He saw that it was good, and he loved every creature.

God gave all the other creatures to human beings. We are to use God's gifts in a way that will give him glory and serve others. Because we can think, choose, and love, we can guard and protect God's creation. We can use each gift in a way that will be good for all.

God wants the gifts of creation to be used for our good. Check the things that you do.

_____ I take time to enjoy the stars, sunset, trees, and water.

___✓___ I plant flowers or vegetables and experience the joy of seeing them grow.

_____ I take care of the birds and my pets by feeding them.

_____ I eat vegetables rather than let them go to waste.

___✓___ I help keep God's creation beautiful by throwing trash in the right places and never littering.

We Are to Value Human Life

God wants his people to care for human life—their own and one another's.

God wants all people to

- be free,
- grow and be happy during their lives here on Earth,
- eat, sleep, and exercise so their bodies will grow,
- see, hear, study, and think so their minds will grow,
- choose to love him and others,
- share in his life,
- pray, and
- walk in his presence.

By doing these things, people will become more like their God. They will be preparing for eternal life with God. They will love what God wants and be happy forever.

Sometimes because they are being selfish God's people forget how special and important life is. God knows the hearts of his people. He knows they sometimes get angry or envious. They take away other people's rights to live and grow. They kill or injure others. They also hurt themselves by misusing alcohol and drugs.

God has given us a commandment that protects life. It is the fifth commandment.

5 You shall not kill.

God gave life. God alone may take it away.

The LORD is my shepherd;
    there is nothing I lack.
In green pastures you let me graze;
    to safe waters you lead me;
    you restore my strength.

You guide me along the right path
    for the sake of your name.
Even when I walk through a dark
    valley,
    I fear no harm, for you are at my
    side;
Only goodness and love
    will pursue me
all the days of my life;
I will dwell in the house of
    the LORD
for years to come.
               Psalm 23:1–4, 6

The Son of God became man because human life is so precious. Jesus wants all people to have everlasting life. His words and deeds showed us how much he values human life. Jesus healed people's bodies and spirits. He fed the hungry and even gave himself as the Bread of Life. He taught people how to love one another. He forbade any word or act that injures or kills the body or the spirit.

Jesus liked to teach in parables. One of these stories was about the Good Shepherd. A shepherd sees that all the sheep get food and exercise and guards them from all harm. Jesus calls himself the Good Shepherd. He tells us:

"A thief comes only to steal and slaughter and destroy; I came so that they might have life and have it more abundantly. I am the good shepherd. A good shepherd lays down his life for his sheep."
               John 10:10–11

We know Jesus is the Good Shepherd because he gave up his life for his sheep. He died on the cross to redeem us so that we could live with him in heaven forever.

Mother Teresa and her sisters went to live in the slums to teach poor children and care for the sick and dying. Because Mother Teresa showed Jesus' love, people wanted to help her. Many more women joined her order.

Mother Teresa's sisters continue the work Jesus did on Earth. The Eucharist is their strength. They take Jesus' love to those whom no one else loves and who have no one else to care for them. No matter how poor the people are, the sisters serve them with Jesus' love. Their care tells these people and all the world that every human life is precious. God in his love has created every person to live with him forever. Every life is a treasure to be guarded.

It isn't easy to take care of people whose bodies are sick and dirty. When the sisters look at these people, they remember that they are the Body of Christ. Because they love Jesus and the gift of life, they can love and care for any person. They find their joy in loving and serving Jesus in his poor.

Mother Teresa Treasured Human Life

The dying elderly man was taken from a roadside ditch. He was washed, fed, and placed on a clean cotton sheet. He did not understand why, but he knew he was being treated with love and respect. He died with happiness in his heart.

The man is one of thousands touched each year by the Missionaries of Charity. This order of sisters was started in 1950 in Calcutta, India, by Mother Teresa. She wanted to take Christ's love to the poorest of the poor.

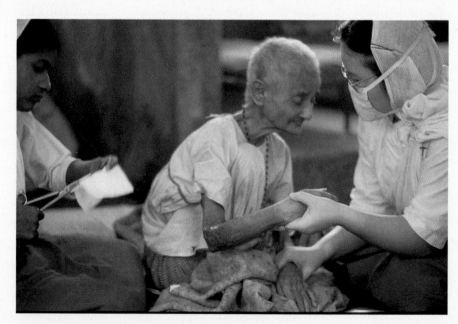

We Care for Our Own Lives

What about you? Do you treasure the gift of life God has given you and others? Right now, you may not be able to do the things Mother Teresa did. But you can treasure the gift of life and keep God's fifth commandment.

If we treasure God's gift of life in ourselves, we will take care of ourselves. We will

* eat good food, exercise, and get enough sleep;
* be careful in games and at work;
* learn to deal with anger;
* use our minds to learn and to think kind thoughts;
* pray and celebrate the sacraments;
* choose friends who will help us to be good; and
* do all that God wants.

We will do nothing that will injure or kill the life of our bodies or our souls. We will not

* injure our bodies on purpose or commit suicide,
* take dares that might endanger our lives,
* use drugs and alcohol so as to weaken our mind's power to think and remember, or
* have anything to do with persons, places, or things that will lead to sin.

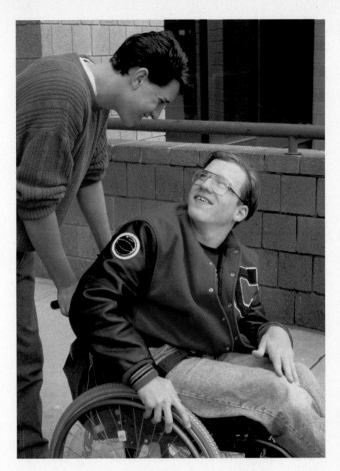

Decide whether the following boys and girls treasure their gift of life. Write **Y** before those who do and **N** before those who do not.

__Y__ Gerardo eats a good breakfast every morning.

__N__ Daniel decided to experiment with drugs to be like some of the older boys he knew.

__Y__ Patrick would not go with the other boys because he knew they planned to torment an old man.

__Y__ Teresa celebrates the Sacrament of Reconciliation each month to grow strong in God's life.

__N__ Stacy rides her bike on the wrong side of the street and does tricks on it.

__Y__ Lisa studies hard and tries to do her best in school.

__Y__ Alex gets enough sleep every night.

We Care for the Lives of Others

Match the statements in the center with the pictures. Place the right number in each box.

Please don't go away angry. We can talk about it.

It would be funny, but I think it might hurt his feelings.

If we all follow the rules, no one will be hurt.

I think I'll shoot baskets until I'm not so angry.

1. We share with others who do not have what they need to live.
2. We speak to build up and not to put down.
3. We forgive and do not hold grudges.
4. We set a good example and do not lead others to sin.
5. We play fair and do not get rough or start fights.
6. We enjoy good fun but do not play unkind jokes.
7. We learn to get rid of our anger without hurting others.
8. We talk about disagreements and do not start fights.

I know you are sorry and I forgive you.

Mary, I'm sure you will be a good player as soon as you get some practice.

Mom, my sweater is too small but is still in good condition. May I give it to someone who needs it?

Tommy, let's leave here. Those children are using bad language.

If we treasure the gift of life, we will respect all people.

People Who Have Disabilities

Every human being has some small disability. Some people have greater ones. Their lives are also precious gifts from God. They have much to share with us.

Elderly, Sick, and Suffering People

People who are old, sick, and suffering are to be treasured. These people remind us of our suffering Savior. They can pray for us. They enrich our lives with their personalities, experiences, and wisdom. We must remember that God gives them life and only God can take it away. *euthanasia - mercy killing*

People Who Are Different

The world is filled with many different kinds of people. There are different races, nationalities, and sexes. Each person is precious and deserves respect. We should try to learn about other people and understand them. Making fun of others or treating them unfairly because they are different is an insult to their Creator.

The fifth commandment forbids anything that does not show respect for life.

Abortion

Abortion, the act of deliberately taking away the life of an unborn baby, is sinful. The life of an unborn baby is to be protected and treasured.

Drugs and Alcohol

Using certain drugs, drinking too much, and smoking endanger not only one's own life but the lives of others.

Reckless Driving

Reckless driving may look like fun on television, but it can hurt and kill people. Life is too precious to take risks with it.

Violence

We see many characters on television using violence to solve problems. As Jesus taught, we must learn to solve our problems peacefully so that no one gets hurt.

Things to Do at Home

1. Go through a Gospel and list ways Jesus showed respect for life.
2. Make a list of the television programs you watch this week that show respect for life. Then list those that do not.
3. Spend some time with one of God's special people. Be aware of the gifts this person has to share. Thank God for the gift of this person's life.
4. Make a poster that promotes life.
5. Compose a prayer for world peace. Mention places in need of peace.

We Remember

What is the fifth commandment?
The fifth commandment is You shall not kill.

Why is human life precious?
Human life is precious because every person is created by God in his image. God gives life; he alone may take it away.

Words to Know

suicide   abortion

We Respond

You knit me in my mother's womb.
I praise you, so wonderfully you made me;
wonderful are your works!

Psalm 139:13–14

We Review

Promote Life! Some puzzle pieces state ways to promote life. Color them green.

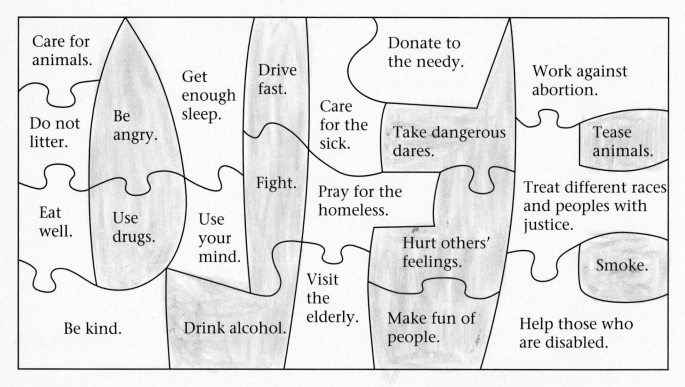

Care for animals.

Do not litter.

Be angry.

Get enough sleep.

Eat well.

Use drugs.

Use your mind.

Be kind.

Drink alcohol.

Drive fast.

Fight.

Care for the sick.

Pray for the homeless.

Visit the elderly.

Donate to the needy.

Take dangerous dares.

Hurt others' feelings.

Make fun of people.

Work against abortion.

Tease animals.

Treat different races and peoples with justice.

Smoke.

Help those who are disabled.

One Boy's Dream Read this true story.

Clinton Hill was only eleven years old when he died of a brain tumor. In his short life he worked hard to protect the environment. Clinton was worried about the air we breathe and water we drink. He dreamed of a worldwide club called Kids for Saving Earth™. After Clinton's death a large chain of stores promoted his ideas during Earth Week in 1990. They made the club known through newspaper ads and commercials. The stores displayed banners with the club's promise and asked people to sign them. These were given to the United Nations General Assembly.

Read the promise on the next page and sign it if you wish.

™Kids for Saving Earth

Kids for Saving Earth™ Promise

Earth is my home. I promise to keep it healthy and beautiful. I will love the land, the air, the water, and all living creatures. I will be a defender of my planet. United with friends, I will help save Earth.

Signature _____

Write one way you will work to save Earth:

_____

_____

_____

™Kids for Saving Earth

God Wants Us to Be Pure and Faithful

Have you ever pulled petals off a flower to find out whether someone loved you? A girl pulls one petal, saying "He loves me," and the next one, saying "He loves me not." She continues until she comes to the last petal, hoping it will end with "He loves me." We do not need a flower to tell us that God loves us. We know he does because he made us and sent his Son to save us. God's love is a faithful love because he has always loved us and always will.

> With age-old love I have loved you.
> Jeremiah 31:3

When God created human beings, he gave them the gift of **sexuality**—he made them male and female. God made men and women equal yet different, planning that couples would love each other deeply and forever. Their love would reflect his total, faithful love for us. God enabled men and women to express this love with their whole being, including their bodies, through their sexuality. In this way, a couple can also share in God's power to bring forth new life.

Because it is related to love and new life, the gift of **sex** is wonderful and good. It should be *a sign of faithful love between two people committed to each other for life.* When it is not, God's plan is not followed, and problems and suffering usually result.

For our protection God gave us two commandments that promote faithful love. The sixth commandment commands married couples to be pure and faithful in love for each other.

6 You shall not commit adultery.

Adultery is giving someone else the love that was promised only to one's marriage partner. It is breaking the marriage vows.

The ninth commandment also safeguards the love between married persons.

> ## 9 You shall not covet your neighbor's wife.

Covet means to desire for ourselves. The ninth commandment means that persons should not desire someone who is married to another person. They should neither plan to be unfaithful to their own partners nor cause someone else to be unfaithful. Married persons should try to build and strengthen their love for their partners.

These two commandments are for everybody, not just for married people. They tell us to respect the gift of our sexuality. By being pure we use sex the way God intended. We treat it with reverence. We do not regard it as a form of entertainment. Instead we make sex a beautiful sign of the special, lasting love we may someday have, for one particular person.

Mary Is Our Model

After Jesus, Mary is the greatest human being. Mary always did God's will. She knew that God's way would be best for all. And so she was a good wife and mother, a woman who lived and loved fully.

One of Mary's titles is Mother Most Pure. As our mother, Mary wants the best for us. She knows the temptations that surround us today, when many people don't value purity. We can pray to Mary to be strong enough to do what is right. She will help us avoid evil and be pure.

Use the code below to find the message.

A –	E – –	H ..–	N ./	R //	V ../
B .	F .–	I – – –	O –/	S ///	W –./
D ...	G .– –	L – –.	P ./.	U –/–	Y –//

/// ..– –/ –./ –// –/ –/– // – –. –/ ../ – –
show your love

.– –/ // .– – –/ ... . –// – – –. –./ – –// ///
for God by always

. – – – – – ./ .– – ./. –/– // – –
being pure.

God Helps Us to Be Pure

Jane is learning to ride a horse at her uncle and aunt's farm. Her aunt Pat is teaching her. "It is most important for you to be in control at all times!" her aunt warns. "Otherwise the horse will do what he wants and will control you!"

Aunt Pat gave Jane some good advice. We can use it also, in another way.

To become the kind of men and women God wants us to be, we must control ourselves and make the right choices. We become strong in **self-control** through practice. Saying no to ourselves is hard. Saying no when other people are saying yes takes courage. We gain control over our lives by saying no to ourselves in small matters. Then, when a serious temptation occurs, we have the power to make the right choice. We are more apt to remain pure. The person who is pure is in control of his or her life.

How would you control your life in the following situations so you could become the person you are called to be?

❖ A friend wants you to watch an X-rated video.
❖ A group on the playground is using "dirty" words that show no respect for sex.
❖ Someone at a party starts telling jokes that make fun of sex.
❖ A classmate passing around a magazine with immodest pictures offers it to you.
❖ Someone suggests playing a game that involves impure acts.

Another means of helping us achieve self-control is prayer. We can ask the Holy Spirit for the gifts of love and courage. We can receive grace to be pure through the Mass and the sacraments. We can pray especially to the Blessed Virgin Mary, our mother, for help. The person who is pure is in control of his or her life.

With the practice of self-control and with prayer, we will have a healthy attitude toward our bodies and the gift of sexuality. We will be able to use this gift to express true love. It will be worth it in this life and the next. As Jesus promised, "Blessed are the clean of heart, for they shall see God" (Matthew 5:8).

God Helps Us to Be Pure

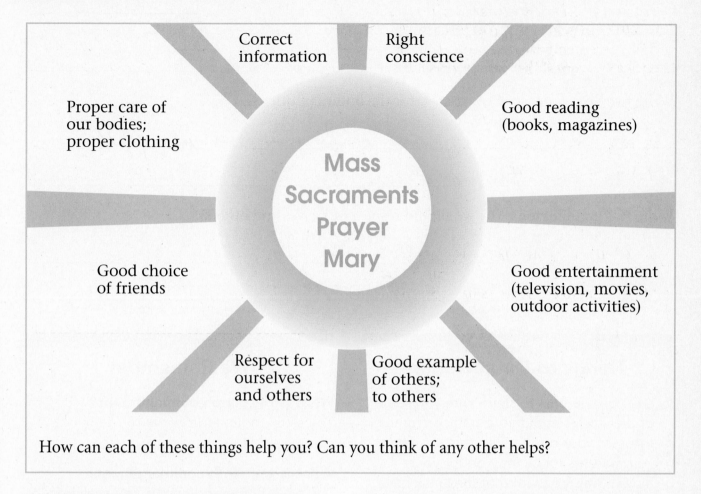

Correct information

Right conscience

Proper care of our bodies; proper clothing

Good reading (books, magazines)

Mass
Sacraments
Prayer
Mary

Good choice of friends

Good entertainment (television, movies, outdoor activities)

Respect for ourselves and others

Good example of others; to others

How can each of these things help you? Can you think of any other helps?

Of all the helps listed in the rays above, there is one we need first: **respect for ourselves and others.** Circle those words in the diagram. If we truly respect ourselves, we will do all the other things necessary to keep ourselves pure.

We are wonderfully made, as only God could make us. Our bodies, with all the powers God gave them, are holy. Our souls are made in the image and likeness of God. Through Baptism, we share in God's life. St. Paul reminds us of this when he says,

 Do you not know that you are the temple of God, and that the Spirit of God dwells in you?

1 Corinthians 3:16

We show respect for a church because it is the house of God. We show respect for our bodies because they are the temples of God.

We show respect for ourselves by the way we care for our bodies and by the way we dress and act. We show it by what we read, look at, listen to, and talk about.

We show respect for others by the way we talk to and about them and by the way we treat them. We must remember that others, too, are temples of God. Jesus himself told us that whatever we do to others we do to him. Stop and think: how have you been treating Jesus lately?

Write two ways you can show respect for your body.

I can *dress and act modestly.*

I can *choose good friends here.*

Write two ways you can show respect for the bodies of others.

I can tell them if there are dangerous thing in a place.

I can stop them from taking drugs.

Write two good reasons why we should respect ourselves and others.

It is a sin to not respect life.

It hurts you and the other person.

Things to Do at Home

1. Ask your parents to share with you some of the stories about your baby pictures or those of your brothers and sisters. Thank your parents for all they do for your family. Pray for them that they may have faithful love.
2. Discuss with your family how all can show respect for one another as temples of God.
3. Many television programs do not show proper respect for married love or for the human body. What can you as a family do about this?
4. Begin the practice of praying a Hail Mary every night for purity.

We Remember

What is the sixth commandment?
The sixth commandment is You shall not commit adultery.

What is the ninth commandment?
The ninth commandment is You shall not covet your neighbor's wife.

Why do we treat our bodies with respect?
We treat our bodies with respect because they are created by God and are temples of the Trinity.

Words to Know
sexuality   sex
adultery

We Respond

Lord, give me the strength I need to be pure in my thoughts, words, and actions.

Crossword Puzzle   Read the clues and write the answers in the puzzle.

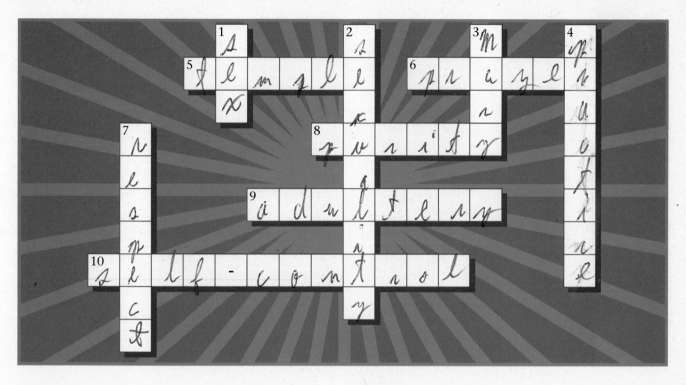

The completed crossword reads: Across 5. EXAMPLE, 6. PRAYER, 8. PURITY, 9. ADULTERY, 10. SELF-CONTROL. Down 1. SEX, 2. SEXUALITY, 3. MARY, 4. PRAYER ROUTINE, 7. RESPECT.

Across

5. We are each a _____ of the Trinity.

6. A means to self-control

8. Using the gift of sex as God intended

9. Giving someone else the love promised to one's marriage partner

10. The power to make oneself carry out a right choice

Down

1. Gift that enables us to express love and bring forth new life

2. Maleness or femaleness

3. A model for purity

4. Same as the clue for 6 Across

7. _____ helps us treat ourselves and others in the right way.

True Love   On each petal write something that can help you love someone someday with true and faithful love.

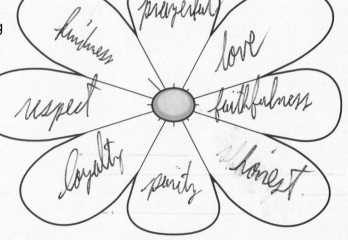

The flower petals read: prayerful, love, faithfulness, honest, purity, loyalty, respect, kindness.

To Own Things Is a Precious Right

Did you ever save up money to buy something you wanted very much? Suppose you took the money and bought a good soccer ball. How would you feel if . . .

someone grabbed your ball and played Keep Away with it?

someone was careless and lost your ball?

someone deliberately made a slit in your ball?

No one has the right to take what belongs to you. No one has the right to destroy or damage it in any way. The right to own things is a gift God has given to every person. The seventh and tenth commandments remind us to respect this gift.

> ### 7 You shall not steal.

The seventh commandment tells us to care for all God's gifts. Whenever we use things or places that belong to others, we must take good care of them. We may not do anything that would spoil or damage them. Neither may we cheat others, for this is stealing.

If we take something that doesn't belong to us, we must return it. If we cannot do this, we must give the owner (or the poor) the money it was worth. If we have damaged something that wasn't ours, we must repair it or make up for the damage. Anytime something has been stolen or damaged, **restitution** must be made. Something must be given to make up for the injustice.

10 You shall not covet anything that belongs to your neighbor.

The tenth commandment reminds us to be satisfied with what we have if we have enough to live with dignity. We should not envy others. We should not resent their having something more, or something better, than we.

What Matters in the End?
The gifts of the earth belong to everyone. Greed is the desire to have more than our fair share of something. The seventh and tenth commandments remind us that we must control our desire for things. We should share when we have something another person needs. How peaceful the world would be if all people respected everyone's right to a fair share of the earth's gifts! *Social Justice*

In Luke 12:16–21 Jesus told a parable about a rich farmer. At harvesttime the man began to worry. "My crops have been good this year," he said to himself. "I don't have a place large enough to store them. What shall I do?" He thought about the problem and decided, "I will tear down my barns and build bigger ones. Then I will have plenty of room for my grain and all my goods. I will say to myself, 'I have all I need for many years. I can take life easy. I can eat, drink, and enjoy myself.'" But God said to him, "You fool! This very night you will die. Then who will get all those good things you have kept for yourself?"

Jesus ended his parable by saying, "This is how it is with those who store up riches for themselves but are not rich in what matters to God."

Why did God call the man a fool?

_____

_____

_____

_____

What would have been a wise decision for the man to make?

_____

_____

_____

_____

_____

To Share What We Own Is a Sacred Duty

Justice is giving everyone what he or she deserves. In a just world, everyone's rights are respected. The weak are protected. The strong try to make life safer and more comfortable for all. Everyone lives in dignity. In the world today many people do not have enough to live comfortably. Other people should provide for their needs and share with them.

Jesus told a story to warn the rich to use their wealth in the right way. You can read the parable in Luke 16:19–31. It tells about a rich man who loved money and the good things money can buy. He refused to share his wealth with Lazarus, a very poor man. The two men died, and Lazarus was carried away by angels to heaven, while the rich man was sent to the torments of hell. He looked up and, seeing Lazarus with Abraham, begged Abraham to have pity and to send Lazarus to comfort him. But Abraham reminded the rich man that during his life he had refused to share with others. Lazarus had suffered much but now

he was at peace. It was impossible to help the rich man. The rich man then begged Abraham to send Lazarus to warn his five brothers. He did not want them to suffer his agony after death. But Abraham answered, "They have Moses and the prophets. Let them listen to them. If they do not listen to them, they will not repent even if someone should rise from the dead."

Do you use everything in a just way? Here are some things God wants us to use justly. Check those you are willing to share.

- ❏ your allowance
- ☑ your clothes
- ❏ your favorite foods
- ❏ playground equipment
- ❏ gifts you receive

Write how you would use one of them in a just way.

I can give them to the poor.

Christians Share Generously with the Poor

Many people do not have proper food, drink, or medical care. Some do not have enough clothes. Others have no education, cannot find work, and do not live in good houses. It is not possible for them to live a decent human life.

True Christians share generously with others. Jesus says, "Whatever you did for one of these least brothers of mine, you did for me" (Matthew 25:40).

A famous story about St. Lawrence and the early Christians teaches us that the poor and needy are truly the treasures of the Church.

Lawrence lived in Rome during the time of the emperor Valerian. As a deacon, Lawrence looked after widows, orphans, and the poor. Christians who had more than they needed gave all they could to the deacons of the Church. Then the deacons found out who needed help and came to their aid.

Emperor Valerian feared the Christians. He ordered that all of them be put to death. When Pope Sixtus II was killed, Lawrence knew that the soldiers would soon be coming for him. He quickly gave all that he had to the poor. Spies were watching Lawrence. They told the governor that the Christians must have great treasures hidden somewhere.

The governor ordered Lawrence arrested. Then he sent for him, hoping to find out where the great treasures were. In a friendly voice, he spoke to Lawrence. "I know that you Christians use silver and gold cups in your worship. You also have many other treasures. The emperor needs them.

Remove them from their hiding place and give them to Caesar. I hear that you want to be fair. Your God doesn't make money. Caesar's stamp is on your coins, so they belong to him. Will you show me where all your treasures are?"

Lawrence's answer pleased the governor. "As you say, our Church is very rich. In fact, no one in the world is richer, not even the emperor. Give me three days to gather the Church's treasures. Then I will bring them to you."

For three days Lawrence walked up and down the streets of Rome. He went to the poor, the sick, and the disabled. On the third day, he brought them all together. He told the governor, "Come, I have all the treasures of the Church. They are ready for you to see."

Can you imagine the governor's anger when he saw all the poor people? He had expected to see shining jewels. Instead he saw people who were hungry and sick. Angrily he asked what this meant. Lawrence replied that the poor and sick were, indeed, the Church's treasures.

The governor ordered Lawrence put to death. Lawrence was to be burned alive. Soldiers chained him to an iron grating and lit a fire beneath it. Lawrence talked and joked with the soldiers. Then he began to pray. He prayed for all the Christians who would be put to death. He prayed that all Romans might become Christians. Soon his painful death was over.

The story of Lawrence's martyrdom spread to faraway lands. Everywhere Christians renewed their devoted care of those in need. They knew that Lawrence was right. The poor *are* the Church's treasures.

Can you tell how these people are bringing justice and showing God's love to others?

❏ Maria's mother refuses to buy products sold by companies that don't pay workers a fair wage.
❏ Tony, a star pitcher, was on a team with some poor losers. He finally quit the team because they destroyed property every time they lost a game.

Write one thing you can do to work for justice.

_____

_____

> "This is how all will know that you are my disciples, if you have love for one another."
>
> John 13:35

Things to Do at Home

1. With your family, decide on three rules you will follow to show that you respect one another's personal things.
2. Look through the newspapers and watch television to find examples of people showing justice as well as injustice.
3. Jesus tells us to use our gifts in the right way. Write how money, food, and school supplies should be used and shared.
4. Print Psalm 37:1–4 and design the borders of your paper.

We Remember

What is the seventh commandment?
The seventh commandment is You shall not steal.

What is the tenth commandment?
The tenth commandment is You shall not covet anything that belongs to your neighbor.

What does Jesus tell us about true riches?
Jesus says, "Store up treasures in heaven. . . . For where your treasure is, there also will your heart be" (Matthew 6:20–21).

Words to Know

restitution   justice
envy

We Respond

Lord, help me to respect all that belongs to others. Give me the love and courage to work so that each person has a fair share of the earth's gifts.

We Review

Acrostic on Justice   Can you fill in the acrostic? Read each sentence and decide which word best completes each one. Then write that word in the acrostic.

1. In a _____ world everyone has enough to live with dignity.

2. Making up for loss of or damage to another's property is called _____.

3. The seventh commandment is You shall not _____.

4. Everyone has the _____ to own things.

5. Every person has a right to enough of the earth's gifts to _____ comfortably.

6. The tenth commandment forbids us to _____ the property of others.

7. _____ people want more than their share of the treasures of the earth.

J u s t
r e s t i t u t i o n
s t e a l
r i g h t
l i v e
c o v e t
g r e e d y

A Just World   In the space around the earth, write things forbidden by the seventh and tenth commandments (for example, stealing). These things have no place in a world of peace and justice.

We Are Builders of Christian Community

Workers who put up a new building need many strong bricks or stones. They need cement to hold the bricks or stones together. They must follow a plan. They must work long and hard to make the building beautiful.

Do you know that the Christian community is like a building? Yes, and we are the builders. St. Paul tells us this when he says:

> We are God's co-workers;
> you are . . . God's building.
> 1 Corinthians 3:9

We build the Christian community with words that are true and kind. Our words are something like the stones in God's building. Our trust in one another and our love for one another are like the cement. Christ's way of life and God's commandments are the special plan we must follow. We too must work long and hard to build up the Christian community.

One of the most important stones to use in God's building is the stone of truthfulness. When we speak the truth, people know they can trust us. When others speak the truth, we know we can trust them. If we do not speak the truth, there will be no trust among us. There will be no Christian community.

To build up trust and love among us, God has given us a special commandment:

8 You shall not bear false witness against your neighbor.

The eighth commandment tells us that we must be truthful, sincere, and kind in our words. It tells us that we must not tell lies, exaggerate, or hurt our neighbor by words. It tells us to keep promises we make and to be faithful in keeping secrets we know.

We can learn about truthfulness from Jesus. He always spoke the truth. He said everything honestly and openly. Everywhere he went, Jesus acted and spoke truthfully. That is why so many people listened to him and trusted him.

Jesus told the truth even when it brought him suffering. When he was asked by Pilate if he was a king, Jesus responded truthfully that he was, indeed, a king.

Jesus loves the truth because he is the Truth. He told us this when he said, "I am the way and the truth and the life" (John 14:6).

Jesus will help us to love the truth if we ask him. He will give us the courage to speak the truth even when it is hard.

Sometimes we find it hard to tell the truth and are tempted to lie. Why might we be tempted to lie? Write some reasons.

To impress your friend.
To avoid punishment.
To get revenge.

When we are tempted to lie, we should pray and ask Jesus to help us. We should ask ourselves the question: Why is it better to tell the truth? Write some good reasons for telling the truth.

To avoid punishment.
A Lie is sinful.
People will trust you.

Jesus gave us a good reason for telling the truth. To find out what it is, start with the top center letter of the circle and skip every other letter. Print the words on the lines below.

The Truth will set you free.

John 8:32

Kind Words Build Up the Christian Community

Kind words are also important stones to use in building up the Christian community. Kind words bring peace and happiness to everyone. They build up love that unites us as a community. St. Paul encourages us to be kind when he says:

Be kind to one another, compassionate, forgiving one another as God has forgiven you in Christ.

Ephesians 4:32

In the eighth commandment, God tells us to be kind in our words. This commandment reminds us that God gave us a gift of great power when he gave us each a tongue. We can use this gift to do much good or much harm. St. James says the tongue is small but powerful, like the rudder of a ship.

If we speak unkind words, we "cut people down" and destroy love in the community. If we speak kind words, we bring happiness to people and build up love.

Jesus shows us how important kind words are. His words were always kind. Often he greeted his friends with "Peace be to you" or "Do not be afraid." To sinners he spoke words of forgiveness. He told us of his love and called us his friends. He told us that he loves us as the Father loves him.

Our words should be kind, like those of Jesus. How can we tell if our words are full of love? St. Paul gives us the answer:

Love is patient, love is kind. It is not jealous, [love] is not pompous, it is not inflated, it is not rude, it does not seek its own interests, it is not quick-tempered, it does not brood over injury, it does not rejoice over wrongdoing but rejoices with the truth.

1 Corinthians 13:4–6

If we are kind, our words will show love for others. Our words will not express jealousy, selfishness, rudeness, or meanness.

In the bricks write kind, courteous words.

Protect Names

The good name, or reputation, of every person is very important. Without a good reputation people find it hard to make friends. They lose the love and respect of others in the Christian community. They may even lose love and respect for themselves and find it hard to love God and others. If we are kind, we do all we can to protect the good names of others. We

- try to think good things about others;
- do not judge what others do, because only God can do that;
- do not spread rumors or say untrue things about others;
- do not gossip about others' sins or faults, even if real;
- do not talk about others behind their backs;
- do not say anything that might embarrass others; and
- do not tell secrets we have promised to keep.

In hurting another person by our words, we hurt ourselves and the whole Christian community.

Sometimes our feelings may tempt us to be unkind. When this happens, we should handle our feelings in a way that will not hurt others.

What are some of the feelings that may tempt us to be unkind? Write them.

envy, hatred, anger
jealous, hurting, imassment,
fear,

We can help ourselves to be kind by looking for the good in others and by saying kind words.

What are some of the good things you have seen others do? Write them.

Say something good about
someone

Can you imagine letting all the feathers in a pillow fly out and then trying to put them all back in? Do you think you could do it? You may say it would be impossible. It is just as difficult to make up to another person when we have harmed his or her good name. But we should do all we can to repair the harm. We should inform those to whom we have spoken that we said something false and unkind. We should ask pardon of the person we have harmed. We should build up respect for him or her by our kindness.

Show Kindness

The Holy Spirit will help us keep God's eighth commandment. This Spirit of truth and love will give us the courage to tell the truth even when it is hard. The Spirit will also help us to be kind in all we say and do. Here is a prayer we can say to the Holy Spirit.

Come, Holy Spirit, fill the hearts of your faithful and kindle in them the fire of your love. Send forth your Spirit and they shall be created and you will renew the face of the earth. Lord, by the light of the Holy Spirit you have taught the hearts of your faithful. In the same Spirit help us to relish what is right and always rejoice in your consolation. We ask this through Christ our Lord. Amen.

Draw cartoons showing how you would be kind in these situations. Use stick figures and put what you would say in balloons.

Your sister Jeannie received a new bike for her birthday. You wish you had one, too, because yours is broken.

Your friend Brad accidentally knocked you down as he was running on the playground.

Just when you wanted to play with your friends, your mother asked you to take care of your baby brother.

The Children of Fatima Kept Their Word

On May 13, 1917, just outside Fatima, Portugal, Lucia and her cousins, Jacinta and Francisco, were watching sheep. Suddenly lightning flashed from the cloudless sky and a ball of light appeared above a small evergreen. In the center of the light stood a beautiful Lady, more brilliant than the sun. Her folded hands held a rosary. She spoke to the children and asked them to come back on the thirteenth of each month for six months.

When the younger children got home, they excitedly told their families about the vision. Lucia's mother, Maria Rosa, thought Lucia was lying. Then the neighbors began to gossip. The family name and honor were being ruined.

Maria Rosa threatened to punish Lucia if she did not confess to lying. Lucia could only plead with her mother that the Lady really had appeared. Maria Rosa did everything to make Lucia admit that she was lying, but she failed. She even took Lucia to the pastor. Now Lucia began to realize what the Lady had meant when she had said, "You will have much to suffer."

Through the following months the neighbors made fun of the three children who saw the Lady. One day the officials took the three children away and locked them in a room. The officials asked the children to tell the secret the Lady had told them, but the children refused.

The children were sent to jail, where they cried and prayed the rosary. The jailer threatened to have Jacinta boiled in oil if she did not tell the secret. He took her away. The other two children prayed for one another and for courage.

The jailer came back for Francisco. "You're next, Lucia," he said, "unless you tell me the secret."

"I would rather die," replied Lucia.

"Very well, you shall," he said.

The jailer came again and took Lucia. When she was brought into the other room, she saw both Jacinta and Francisco alive and well. How happy they were to be safe!

The three children did not tell the secret. The officials could do nothing more, so they took the children back to Fatima. That same day the children saw our Lady and spoke to her.

Looking for the Truth

Read the questions and write the answers.

Why was Lucia's mother angry with her?

She thought Lucia lying

What harm was done by the neighbors' gossip?

It ruined the family name

Why were the three children so brave?

They prayed for courage and they new they were telling the truth.

What should you do when you are tempted to lie or break a promise?

I should just tell the truth

Things to Do at Home

1. Discuss: How does the eighth commandment help your family be a happy one? Why should you protect another's good name?

2. Play the Telephone Game with your family or friends to show how truth can be changed. Have one person whisper a message to another person. The message is passed on until everyone has received it. The last person should say it aloud so that it can be compared to the original message.

3. Say a prayer to the Holy Spirit and ask him to help you speak only true and kind words.

We Remember

What is the eighth commandment?
The eighth commandment is You shall not bear false witness against your neighbor.

What are we commanded by the eighth commandment?
We are commanded by the eighth commandment to speak the truth and to be kind in our words.

We Respond

Come, Holy Spirit, fill the hearts of your faithful and kindle in them the fire of your love.

We Review

A Truth Text   Answer these questions.
Why is it wrong to forge your parent's signature?

You'er, only hurting your self. It's a lie. It dishonest. It is also against the

Why is it wrong to copy someone's homework?

It cheating and a lie.

Why shouldn't we gossip about someone's faults?

It's none of your busness

Truth

Be Builders of Community   Write the letter *B* before the phrases that tell what builds the community. Write *D* before those that tell what destroys community.

_B_ **1.** A truth spoken with love

_D_ **2.** A lie that damages a good name

_B_ **3.** A word of sympathy

_D_ **4.** An insult that hurts another

_D_ **5.** A lie that causes trouble

_D_ **6.** A broken promise

_B_ **7.** A word of forgiveness

_D_ **8.** An act of cheating

_D_ **9.** A lie that blames another

_B_ **10.** A word of friendly advice

_B_ **11.** An honest word of praise

_D_ **12.** A truth that damages a good name

_D_ **13.** A judgment without reason

_B_ **14.** An encouraging word

_D_ **15.** An exaggeration that starts a rumor

_B_ **16.** A pleasant greeting

Christians Serve as Jesus Did

People belong to either the I-team or the U-team. Those on the I-team make statements like these:

✤ I want it.
✤ What's in it for me?
✤ It's mine!
✤ I don't want to do it!

People on the U-team speak this way:

✤ It's for you.
✤ No problem. I'll be glad to do it.
✤ May I get it for you?
✤ Let me help you.

Do you think only about yourself? Or do you really care about others? To which team do you belong?

Jesus told a parable that teaches us that we must serve one another. He reminded us that every time we do good to others, we show our love for him. Read that parable from your New Testament, Matthew 25:31–46.

Here are some **works of mercy.**

 A. Feed the hungry.
 B. Visit the sick.
 C. Give drink to the thirsty.
 D. Welcome the stranger.
 E. Clothe the naked.
 F. Warn the sinner.
 G. Instruct the ignorant.
 H. Give advice to those in doubt.
 I. Comfort those in sorrow.
 J. Pray for those in need.

Jesus spent his whole life giving to others. He said, "Whoever wishes to be great among

you shall be your servant. . . . The Son of Man did not come to be served but to serve" (Matthew 20:26–28).

Write the letter of the work of mercy that Jesus performed. Give the story a title.

__E__ **1.** John 2:1–11
The wedding at Cana

__H__ **2.** Matthew 5:1–12
Sermon at the Mount

__I__ **3.** John 17:9–11
The Prayer of Jesus

__A__ **4.** Luke 9:10–17
Jesus feeds the hungry

__H__ **5.** Mark 10:17–27
Give advice to those who doubt

We all want to stand at Jesus' right hand at the last judgment. We must begin now to see people in need and to help them. We will find people who are hungry or sick, in doubt or in sorrow, right at home. We can perform many acts of service.

Choose three works of mercy from page 171 and tell how you can practice them.

Work _Pray for those in need_

Practice _Pray in class_

_____

Work _Warn the sinner_

Practice _I can tell the sinner_
what is the right thing

Work _Comfort those in sorrow_

Practice _____

_____

Mercy Match

Can you match these activities with the works of mercy listed on page 171? Place the letter of the work of mercy before the statement.

_a_ 1. Vince helps his mother in the soup kitchen.

_I_ 2. Erica is teaching her little sister the alphabet.

_D_ 3. Karl introduced the new boy to his coach.

_d_ 4. Alex prays that there will soon be world peace.

_B_ 5. Jane went with her father to visit her aunt, who had just come home from the hospital.

_I_ 6. When José got home from school, he found his mother crying. He went over to her and gave her a big hug.

_E_ 7. The safety patrol captain reported some children who would not follow the safety rules when they rode their bikes to school.

_H_ 8. Suzi wondered if she should go shopping with a certain group of girls. When Beth reminded Suzi that these girls often shoplift, Suzi decided not to go.

_d_ 9. Heidi knew that Angela's grandfather had just died. She prayed for him before she went to bed.

_E_ 10. Marcy and her mother took her little brother's clothes to Mrs. Thomas for her new baby.

Martin De Po[rres] [Lo]ved Others

Don Juan de Porres looked down at his newborn son. The baby was black, like his mother. Don Juan had wanted a son who looked like a Spanish nobleman. He was not happy and soon left his wife and children.

Seven years later Don Juan had reason to visit Lima, Peru, again. He heard people talking about an unusual eight-year-old boy. "Everybody loves Martin, señor. He is so kind. He cannot pass a beggar without giving him something. He would rather go hungry or even let his mother beat him."

Don Juan grew pale as he learned more about this boy. It was Martin, his son, the one he had looked down on! A short time later he met Martin. Hearing of his great desire to learn to read and write, Don Juan agreed to send him to school. Blacks were not permitted to go to school in Lima. Don Juan took his son to the place where he lived and enrolled him in school.

Later, Martin returned to Lima. With the help of a wealthy woman, he went to work for a prominent doctor. While there he learned how to cure many illnesses.

Martin worked in patients' homes, hospitals, and the doctor's home. He soon became skilled in healing people. He became famous. People from different places sent for Martin when they were sick.

"Send for Martin," pleaded a slave.

"My father has been badly wounded," a young Indian girl cried. "Will you come and save him?"

"I am a sick and dying man. Bring Brother Martin to me," the governor ordered.

Soon Martin wanted to give himself completely to God. He made vows and became a Dominican brother. He continued to work among the poor and sick. His love and kindness inspired others to help.

"Brother Martin, here is half my fortune to help build a house for homeless children."

"Here is some money, Brother. Take it to buy food for your poor patients."

Martin bandaged the wounds of the sick. He stayed at their bedsides through nights of fever and pain. When someone died who could not afford a funeral, Martin buried that person himself. He sold his broad-brimmed hat to buy bread for two prisoners.

The people of Lima and the nearby towns loved Martin very much. They thought of him as a saint long before he died.

Brother Martin served others in the name of Jesus. He brought them Jesus' love and care. When he died, how happy he must have been to see Jesus!

A World of Love Puzzle

Use the clues and the words in the picture of the world to work the puzzle.

Across

1. God wants us to be faithful to our _____.

2. Jesus showed us how to love God and _____.

6. God's fifth commandment tells us to protect all _____.

7. God's seventh and tenth commandments tell us to be _____ in sharing our gifts with others.

9. The eighth commandment tells us to speak words that are kind and _____.

Down

1. God wants us to _____ our own life and the lives of others.

3. To be just and kind, we _____ what we have with others.

4. The sixth and ninth commandments tell us to be _____ and faithful in love.

5. Our words bring peace and happiness when they are true and _____.

8. Sharing with the poor and suffering people helps to make a _____ world.

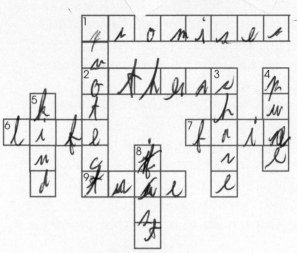

promises
pure   fair
just   true   kind
life   share
protect   others

Search for a Message from Jesus

P	L	R	O	V	B	Q	E	Z	O	X	S	Q	N	H	E	A	S
P	N	D	O	X	Z	Q	T	M	H	E	S	X	R	K	P	A	C
S	Q	F	Q	I	G	X	P	K	L	Q	S	P	O	M	X	V	A
E	X	K	Y	Q	C	O	P	S	U	X	Z						

1. Cross out every third letter.

2. Cross out every *P*, *Q*, and *X*.

3. On the lines below, print the letters that are left.

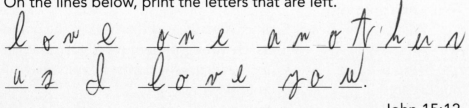

love one another
as I love you.

John 15:12

Looking Back at Unit 5

In this unit you have learned about God's commandments of love for others. Jesus showed us by his words and actions how we are to love others. You have seen his example of loving and protecting life as well as his purity, honesty, and truthfulness. You have read how the saints followed his example and kept God's laws, living in love.

Your study of the works of mercy has shown you how we can serve others in our daily lives. You have been reminded of Jesus' words, "Whatever you did for one of these least brothers of mine, you did for me" (Matthew 25:40).

You have learned that, by living in love, you will have joy in this life and eternal life in heaven.

Living the Message

In what ways do you show you live in love? Write your answers on the lines.

1. I show my love to others by
telling them they are useful.

2. I am patient and kind to others when
they are kind to me

3. I love and protect life by
letting no human get to it.

4. I show respect for others' property when
I walk on the sidewalk

5. I speak the truth whenever
I am sad.

6. I protect my purity by
not taking drugs.

Planning to Grow

Draw stick figures in each block to show something you will do to keep God's laws.

I Respect Life	I Protect My Purity	I Share My Things	I Speak the Truth

Lord, Teach Us to Serve

Introduction

Leader 1: A certain young man asked Jesus what he should do to gain eternal life. Jesus told him to keep the commandments. The young man said he had kept the commandments from the time he was a boy. Jesus invited him to go a step further. He told the young man to sell his belongings, take care of the poor, and then follow him.

Leader 2: Jesus invites each of us to keep the commandments and then do more. He wants us to give service to his people. He wants us to give them food and friendship. He wants us to teach them, comfort them, and help them. He tells us that the road of service is the road he travels. It is the road to heaven. Let us pray now that we will be generous in giving service.

Song

Reading *(Matthew 25:31–46, adapted)*

Reader 1: In Palestine, sheep and goats used to graze together. When it was time to move them to other pastures, the sheep were separated from the goats. Jesus used this example to give us an important message.

Reader 2: The story takes place at the end of time: Christ's second coming. All people are gathered before him. As a shepherd separates his goats and sheep, so Jesus separates the people into two groups: the good people on his right and the evil ones on his left. First he speaks to those on his right.

Jesus: Come, you who are blessed by my Father. Inherit the kingdom prepared for you from the foundation of the world. For I was hungry and you gave me food, I was thirsty and you gave me drink, a stranger and you welcomed me, naked and you clothed me, ill and you cared for me, in prison and you visited me.

Reader 1: Then the just persons will say,

Person 1: Lord, when did we see you hungry and give you food?

Person 2: When did we see you thirsty and give you drink?

Person 3: When did we welcome you?

Person 4: When did we clothe you?

Person 5: When did we visit you when you were sick or in prison?

Reader 2: Jesus will answer them,

Jesus: I tell you, that as often as you did it for any of my brothers and sisters, you did it for me.

Reader 2: Then the Lord will say to those on his left,

Jesus: Depart from me and go into the eternal fire prepared for the devil and his angels. For I was hungry and you gave me no food, I was thirsty and you gave me no drink, a stranger and you gave me no welcome, naked and you gave me no clothing, ill and in prison, and you did not care for me.

Reader 1: Then the condemned persons will say,

Condemned People: When did we see you and not take care of your needs?

Jesus: When you refused to help my brothers and sisters, you refused to help me.

Reader 2: These will suffer eternal punishment, and the just will have eternal life.

Prayer

Leader 2: Many followers of Christ are taking care of the needy. Let us praise God who gives them his love. Please respond: We praise you, Lord.

Leader 1: For those who feed the hungry . . .

For those who give drink to the thirsty . . .

For those who visit the sick . . .

For those who welcome the stranger . . .

For those who give clothes to the poor . . .

For those who help sinners to be sorry for their sins . . .

For those who teach others to know God . . .

For those who comfort people in sorrow . . .

For those who forgive injuries . . .

For those who pray for people in need . . .

Leader 2: Lord, we give you ourselves.
Help others through us.

Leader 1: Please respond: Teach us to
show them your love.

Lord, many of our brothers and
sisters are hungry and thirsty . . .
Lord, many of your people are sick or
in prison . . .
Lord, so many people do not know
you or your Gospel . . .
Lord, many people you love are
lonely and in sorrow . . .
Lord, many of your people have
sinned and do not know of your
love and forgiveness . . .
Let us gather our prayers and praise
together as we say the prayer that
Jesus taught us. Our Father . . .

All: God our Father, forgive our sins. Give
us new life and hope. Grant that we
may share your love and peace with
everyone we meet. We ask this in
Jesus' name. Amen.

Song

FAMILY FEATURE

Ethiopian Bread

Alemaz Abebe and her family are proud to be from Ethiopia, for this was the earliest Christian land in East Africa. She grew up eating *injera*, the national bread of Ethiopia, which is served with almost every meal. Injera is a kind of firm pancake that is used as a plate and spoon. The Abebes place food like spicy stew on injera. Then they break off pieces of injera and use them to scoop up the food.

For a special treat, your family may enjoy injera. Making it can be a family project. As you eat it, think of millions of Christians all over the world who like you survive by bread and the sacred bread of the Eucharist. Think of the many people who have little more than bread to eat. Discuss how you can contribute to organizations like Food for the Poor and Bread for the World, which work to feed the hungry.

Injera

5 tablespoons all-purpose flour	3 1/2 cups club soda
3 cups pancake mix	at room temperature
1/4 teaspoon baking soda	1 1/2 cups of water

Combine flour, pancake mix, and baking soda in a bowl. Pour in club soda and water steadily, stirring constantly. When mixture is smooth and thin, strain it through a fine sieve over another bowl. Warm a ten-inch skillet over moderate heat until it will set the batter without browning it. Test the pan by pouring a tablespoon of batter onto it. The bottom should solidify immediately without turning brown. For each injera, remove the pan from the heat and ladle in 1/4 cup batter. Tip pan until bottom is covered. Cover pan partially and cook bread over moderate heat for one minute or until the top is spongy, moist, and dotted with airholes. The bottom should be smooth, dry, a little shiny, and not brown. Remove the pan from the heat and remove the injera.

God's Law

Decide which commandment someone is keeping or breaking.
Write its number on the line.

10
_____ **1.** Jim saw Margaret playing with the latest popular
video game cartridge. Her brother gave it to her for
her birthday. Jim wanted the game very much and
had only a little money saved to buy it. He resented
that she was given the game and did not have to save
to buy it.

7
_____ **2.** Anne and Julie were two popular girls in school.
When Jane moved to their neighborhood, she wanted
to be their friend. Anne and Julie told her that she
could be their friend if she stole some things for them
at the store. Jane knew this was wrong and decided
she would rather find other friends.

8   **3.** Joe took some markers from Conor and kept them for himself. George saw his best friend, Joe, take the markers. When the teacher asked where the markers were, George said another student took them.

1   **4.** The king of England pressured St. Thomas More to take an oath declaring the king the head of Church or he would be killed. Thomas refused because he knew it wasn't true.

6   **5.** St. John the Baptist pointed out that it was wrong for King Herod to marry his brother's wife. For this, John was beheaded.

7   **6.** St. Augustine is a great bishop and doctor of the Church. When he was a boy, he and some friends helped themselves to some pears from a neighbor's orchard.

5   **7.** Twelve-year-old St. Maria Goretti was alone in the house when a boy who worked on the property came in and wanted her to commit a sexual sin with him. When Maria refused, he stabbed her to death.

(Answers: 1. 10, 2. 7, 3. 8, 4. 1, 5. 6, 6. 7, 7. 5)

SUPPLEMENT

We Worship God throughout the Year

We Celebrate the Feast of All Saints

Many saints have a special feast day. Usually on the anniversary of their death, we honor them with a celebration. These and all other saints are remembered on the Feast of All Saints. If members of your family have died and are with God, this is their feast day too. You have special cause to rejoice and celebrate.

We hope to be with the saints in heaven someday. Learning how these people lived can help us to follow Jesus. Every saint felt hurt, lonely, and frightened at times, just as we do. They sometimes failed to do God's will. They sinned because, like us, they were weak, but they were sorry for their sins and kept on trusting in God's love. They knew God loved them and wanted them to be his special friends. They listened to God and talked to him each day in prayer.

The saints served God in many different ways. Some saints loved God in a special way from the time they were little children. Other saints were great sinners before they turned to God.

Some saints had important jobs as Church leaders or leaders of their countries. The good works of other saints were hidden, known only to their family and friends.

Every saint, whether young or old, rich or poor, loved God more than anyone or anything else. Each saint served God and others by using his or her talents.

It was hard for the saints to be kind when they were angry. It was not easy for them to say no when their friends wanted them to do something wrong. But, because the saints loved God very much, they did good even when it was hard.

How glad they must be now for all the times they were unselfish and faithful to God, for he has brought them to the unending joys of heaven. On the Feast of All Saints we ask them to help us serve God faithfully until death. We ask our favorite saints to watch over us with special love.

Name the Saints

Can you name the saints in the riddles? Use the code below if you need help. Print the letters of each name on the lines.

Code

A	B	C	D	E	F	H	I	L	M	N	O	P	R	S	T	U	V	X	Y
1	2	3	4	5	6	7	8	9	10	11	12	13	14	15	16	17	18	19	20

Riddles

Answers

1. I was a poor and sickly French girl. Our Lady appeared to me at Lourdes. I prayed much for sinners.

Bernadette
2 5 14 11 1 4 5 16 16 5

2. I was a great missionary. After I heard Ignatius Loyola say, "What does a man gain if he wins the whole world and loses his soul?" I became a Jesuit.

Francis
6 14 1 11 3 8 15

Xavier
19 1 18 8 5 14

3. I am a Carmelite saint. My Little Way shows how offering joys and sorrows daily can make great saints.

Thérèse
16 7 5 14 5 15 5

4. I was the chancellor for King Henry VIII in England. When I refused to say he was the head of the Church, he had me beheaded. My last words were, "I die the king's good servant but God's first."

Thomas More
16 7 12 10 1 15   10 12 14 5

5. I was the first American citizen to be declared a saint. I worked especially with people who came from Italy to the United States.

Frances
6 14 1 11 3 5 15

Cabrini
3 1 2 14 8 11 8

Write your own riddle. Figure out the code for the answer.
See whether others can guess your saint.

_____

_____

_____

_____

Advent Is a Time of Waiting

A Time of Waiting Is a Time of Preparing
Item from the *Happyday Herald*

Waitmore City—David Wise has been looking forward to a visit from his best friend, Marty Bell. David's wish almost came true last week when he received a letter from Marty that said he would be coming Sunday to spend a week with David. Because of the heavy snowstorms, however, Marty has not been able to travel. Meanwhile, David is eagerly making plans for all the things he and his friend will do.

David was certain his friend would come soon. He used his time of waiting to prepare for the visit. He planned how they would celebrate together.

The people of God had to wait a long time for the coming of the Savior. After the fall of our first parents, God promised to send a Savior. The prophets reminded the people of God's promise. They told where, when, and how the Redeemer would come. They urged the people to pray, prepare, and plan how they would celebrate the Savior's coming.

Some people got tired of waiting. They did not prepare for Jesus' coming. They did not recognize him when he finally came! Those people who trusted in God's promise continued to prepare for the Savior. Their longing and waiting were rewarded when the Son of God came to earth some two thousand years ago.

The Church gives us the four weeks before Christmas to prepare for the coming of Jesus. This time is called **Advent.** Advent is a time to look into our hearts to see whether there is anything that would stand in the way of Jesus' coming. It is also a time to think of the real meaning of Christmas.

Jesus already came in *history.* He also comes to us in *grace* each time we pray. He comes to us in the people we meet and live with. He comes in the happenings of every day. He asks us to show our love for him and others by being his witnesses. Only if we pray and wait for him will we know him in his many comings.

Finally, Advent is a time to remind ourselves to prepare for the final coming of Christ in *glory.* At that time he will judge the living and the dead, and call us to our eternal reward. In order to share his life in heaven we must prepare for his coming by living and loving as he did.

As we eagerly wait for a new coming of Christ into our lives, how can we prepare? Does your family do anything special to prepare for Jesus' coming at Christmas, such as make an Advent wreath or follow an Advent calendar?

Complete each sentence by writing the correct "coming." The words are on this page. Then match the sentence number with the symbol of that coming.

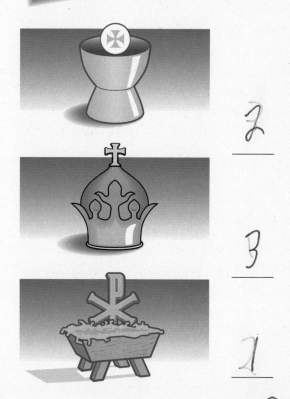

1. Jesus came to earth almost two thousand years ago. He came in
   a baby history .

2. Jesus comes to us in the Eucharist. He comes in the happenings of every day. He comes in
   prayer grace .   **3**

3. Jesus will come on the last day to judge all people. He will come in
   spir glory .   **1**

Mary and John the Baptist Prepared in a Special Way

God asked Mary and John the Baptist to prepare for his Son's coming in a special way. If reporters could have written the story for the newspapers, it might have looked like this:

Nazareth News—Evening Edition, March 25
Early this morning a heavenly messenger came to Nazareth. The angel Gabriel visited Mary, daughter of Anne and Joachim of the family of David. His mission was to deliver a message from God the Father. Mary was asked to be the mother of God's Son. At first Mary was frightened and worried. Gabriel told her the power of God would come upon her.

With love and joy, Mary accepted God's will for her. She told the angel that God could do as he wished with her life; she was his handmaid. At this moment she became the Mother of God.

Mary has also heard that her older relative Elizabeth will have a child. Mary will go to Judea to help her. Early tomorrow morning she will leave with Jacob Bar Jonah's caravan. We wish her a pleasant journey.

When we spoke to Mary this afternoon, she seemed full of deep peace and joy. She said she had always prayed to be the Lord's handmaid. Our best wishes are with her as she takes on her new duties as Mother of God!

Jordan Journal—Evening Edition
From the banks of the Jordan a voice can be heard calling, "Prepare a way for the Lord!" The voice is that of a young man who has just completed a forty-day fast in the desert. He claims to be the one chosen to prepare the way for the coming of the Messiah. He is John the Baptist, son of Zechariah and Elizabeth.

When asked how to prepare, John tells the people to repent and to change their lives. He also tells the soldiers to be satisfied with their pay. He warns them not to push people around or blame them for something they didn't do!

John baptizes the people with water. He promises that One will come who will baptize with the Holy Spirit—One greater than he is who will bring the Good News of salvation. Who can this be? We'll just have to wait and see. John seems to think he'll be along any day now. Join us at the Jordan tomorrow. Get ready for the coming of the Lord.

Compare these news reports with the Gospel stories of Mary (Luke 1:26–38) and John (Luke 3:2–18).

Things to Do at Home

1. Have a family meeting. Decide what you as a family will do to prepare for the coming of Christ. You might plan a family "Keep Christ in Christmas" campaign.
2. Read the Gospel stories of Mary and John the Baptist on page 184. Discuss how they prepared for the Lord and how family members can imitate them.
3. Do one thing this evening to show Jesus you are eager for his coming.

We Remember

What is Advent?
Advent is a time of waiting and preparing for the coming of Jesus. We think about his coming in history. We prepare for his coming in grace and for his final coming in glory.

We Respond

Come, Lord Jesus, come!

We Review

Prepare His Way Fill in the puzzle by printing the correct word to complete each sentence. The number of blanks will give you a clue to the missing word.

One of the best ways to prepare for Jesus is to P _l_ _a_ _y_.

John told the people to make up for sin and to R _e_ _p_ _e_ _n_ _t_.

During Advent we should be preparing our _h_ E _a_ _r_ _t_ _s_.

People who kept alive the promise of a Savior were P _r_ _o_ _p_ _h_ _e_ _t_ _s_.

The woman chosen to be Jesus' mother was _M_ A _r_ _y_.

Jesus came to earth as our _S_ _a_ _v_ _i_ _o_ R.

Jesus comes to us now in _g_ _r_ _a_ _c_ E.

Jesus Christ came to earth 2,000 years ago in H _i_ _s_ _t_ _o_ _r_ _y_.

Christ died to save us from death and from _S_ I _n_.

John was known as the _B_ _a_ _p_ _t_ _i_ S _t_.

As baptized Christians we must give Christlike W _i_ _t_ _n_ _e_ _s_ _s_.

The four weeks before Christmas are called A _d_ _v_ _e_ _n_ _t_.

Jesus will come again in _g_ _l_ _o_ _r_ Y.

185

We Celebrate Lent

Lent Is a Time for Change

The word *lent* comes from an old English word that means "springtime." **Lent**, the forty days before Easter, is the springtime of our spiritual lives. In spring the many changes we see in nature are signs that new life is coming to earth. The changes we make during Lent to become more like Jesus are signs that his life is growing in us.

During Lent we let the warmth of God's love touch us and fill our hearts. We open ourselves to the Lord through increased prayer and acts of self-denial. We change whatever is selfish in our lives. We think more about Jesus, who has taught us the meaning of true love: being willing to sacrifice even our lives for those we love.

Jesus spoke about the mystery of a dying seed. He said,

 "Unless a grain of wheat falls to the ground and dies, it remains just a grain of wheat; but if it dies, it produces much fruit."

John 12:24

When Jesus gave up his life on the cross, he rose to a new and glorious life. He shares that life with us when we are baptized. This life grows as we share in the death and resurrection of Jesus. Lent gives us the chance to become more like Jesus. Our Lenten practices help us to become more unselfish and to share more fully in the life of Jesus.

We Follow Jesus during Holy Week

During Holy Week we recall the greatest events in the life of our Lord and King. Everyone who loves Jesus tries to follow him on the road to Calvary. One way we can follow him is by taking part in the liturgies of Holy Week.

Passion Sunday (Palm Sunday)

The liturgy of Passion Sunday begins with a procession recalling Jesus' triumphal entry into Jerusalem. It includes the reading of Christ's Passion. Palms are carried in procession and taken home to be put behind a crucifix. Whenever we see the palms, we can acclaim Jesus as our king by saying,

Praise and honor to you, Lord Jesus Christ,
King of endless glory!

Holy Thursday

Holy Thursday

On Holy Thursday, at the Evening Mass of the Lord's Supper, we thank Jesus for his great gifts. We remember how, at the Last Supper, Jesus gave himself to us as our food in the Eucharist and made his apostles priests. On Holy Thursday morning (or earlier in Holy Week) the bishop usually has a Chrism Mass in the cathedral. The oils are blessed, and the priests renew their promise to serve God's people.

At the Last Supper Jesus gave us the new commandment: "Love one another as I love you." He also did something to show us what this means: he washed his apostles' feet. In some parishes the priest reminds us of Jesus' command by washing the feet of twelve people during the Mass of the Lord's Supper. After this Mass, the priest carries the Blessed Sacrament in procession to the place of reposition. People may adore Jesus in the Blessed Sacrament until midnight.

Good Friday

Good Friday

The day on which Jesus suffered and died is called *good* because on that day he saved the world from sin and death. Although there is no Mass on Good Friday, people gather in the afternoon for special services. These services include the reading of the Passion and prayers asking that Jesus' sacrifice save all people. The cross is venerated and kissed by all who wish. Then Holy Communion is distributed.

Under each symbol, write the name of the day of Holy Week it represents. Be ready to tell why it is a symbol for that day.

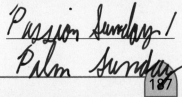

Passion Sunday / Palm Sunday

We Celebrate the Lord's Passion

Scene One

Reader: After the Last Supper, Jesus and the apostles entered the Garden of Gethsemane.

Jesus: Sit here while I go off to pray. Peter, James, John, you come too. Stay awake and pray with me.

(Goes a short distance and kneels.) Father, if it is possible, take this suffering away from me. Not my will but yours be done.

(Returns to apostles, who are asleep.) Peter, could you not watch with me for one hour? Watch and pray that you may not be tested.

(Goes a short distance and kneels.) Father, if this suffering cannot pass, your will be done.

(Returns to find his disciples asleep.) Get up. Let us go. The person who is going to betray me is near.

Judas *(enters with soldiers and kisses Jesus)*: Hail, Master.

Jesus: Friend, do you betray me with a kiss?

(Soldiers take hold of Jesus.)

Peter *(Waving a sword)*: Leave it to me, Master. I will save you.

Jesus: Peter, put your sword away. My Father could send armies of angels to defend me. *(To soldiers)* You have come with swords and clubs to arrest me as if I were a robber. Yet, when I was teaching, you never laid a hand on me. But this is your hour of darkness.

Scene Two

Reader: Jesus was brought before the high priest, Caiaphas, and accused by false witnesses. At the same time, in the courtyard, Peter joined people warming themselves at the fire.

First Accuser: I heard you say that we must not pay taxes to Caesar.

Second Accuser: He has broken the laws of our religion and even works on the Sabbath. He claims he is God's Son.

Caiaphas *(to Jesus)*: Have you anything to say?

(Jesus is silent.)

Woman *(in a loud whisper to Peter)*: You were with the man Jesus.

Peter: I was not.

Third Accuser: This man threw people out of the Temple. He said he could destroy it and in three days rebuild it.

Second Woman *(to Peter)*: You are one of his followers. You talk like him.

Peter: I don't know anything about him.

Caiaphas: Answer. Are you God's Son?

Servant *(to Peter)*: I'm sure you are one of his followers. I've seen you with him.

Peter: I tell you, I don't know the man.

Jesus: You ask me whether I am the Son of God. It is as you say.

Caiaphas: You hear him. He calls himself God. What is the verdict?

All: He must be put to death!

Reader: As Jesus was led out, he looked at Peter with love and forgiveness. Peter went out and cried.

Scene Three

Reader: Jesus was put on trial before Pilate. Caiaphas, other priests, and soldiers were present.

Pilate: What charge do you bring against this man?

Caiaphas: He is a criminal, or we would not have brought him to you.

Pilate: Take him and judge him according to your own laws.

Caiaphas: We don't have the power to put anyone to death.

Pilate: Does he deserve death?

Caiaphas: He has roused the people by saying he is king.

Pilate *(to Jesus)***:** Are you king of the Jews?

Jesus: My kingdom is not of this world. If it were, my servants would be fighting for me.

Pilate: Are you a king, then?

Jesus: It is as you say. I am a king. I came into the world to proclaim the truth.

Pilate: I find nothing wrong with this man. I will just have him scourged.

(Soldiers lead Jesus away.)

Caiaphas: If you let him go, you are no friend of Caesar.

Pilate: You have a tradition of receiving back a prisoner at the Passover feast. Shall I release Jesus? Or Barabbas?

All: Barabbas, not this one.

Pilate: But Barabbas is a murderer.

All: We want Barabbas! We want Barabbas!

Pilate: What shall I do with Jesus?

All: Crucify him!

(Jesus is led in with crown of thorns and scarlet cloak.)

Pilate: Look at the man!

All: Crucify him! Crucify him!

Pilate: Shall I crucify your king?

All: We have no king but Caesar.

(Two servants enter with basin and water.)

Pilate *(washing hands)***:** I wash my hands of the blood of this innocent man.

Scene Four

Reader: Jesus was led out of Pilate's house. A large cross was placed upon his shoulders. People mocked and laughed at him. He walked the rough road to Calvary, carrying his cross. When he could no longer do it alone, the soldiers forced a man named Simon to help carry the cross. Once Jesus reached the hill, the soldiers pulled off his garments. They nailed him to his cross. Upon the cross were the words "Jesus the Nazarene, King of the Jews."

Jesus: Father, forgive them. They don't know what they are doing. *(To Mary)* Mother, behold your son. *(To John)* This is your mother. I thirst.

(Soldier puts sponge on stick and holds it up to Jesus.)

Jesus: It is finished. *(Bows head and dies)*

(The room darkens.)

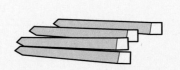

We Celebrate New Life at Easter

The Easter Vigil

Spring is the time when we see all nature rising to new life. It reminds us of the new life we received at Baptism. We begin to celebrate this new life at the Easter Vigil Service on Holy Saturday night.

In the Service of Light, a new fire is made and blessed by the priest. The paschal candle is lighted from this new fire that shines out in the darkness. The Easter candle stands for the risen Jesus, who leads us by the light of his truth. We light our small candles from the paschal candle to show that we can be a light to others by being like Christ. We listen to the great Easter Proclamation:

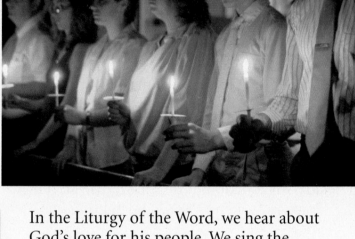

It is truly right that we should praise you, God.

This is the night you saved your people and led them to safety.

This is the night when Christians everywhere are freed from sin and restored to grace.

This is the night when Jesus Christ broke the chains of death and rose triumphant from the grave.

The power of this holy night brings joy, light, peace, and love to all people.

So, Father, we offer joyful praises to you.

In the Liturgy of the Word, we hear about God's love for his people. We sing the *Alleluia,* which means "Praise God." We rejoice with our risen Lord.

The priest blesses water and lowers the Easter candle into it. In the Liturgy of Baptism and Confirmation, we welcome new members into the Church. We renew the promises we made at Baptism and are sprinkled with the blessed holy water.

In the Liturgy of the Eucharist, the newly baptized join us in offering the sacrifice of Jesus to the Father. With us they receive the risen Jesus in Holy Communion.

Easter Sunday

Jesus is risen! Suppose you were living in Jerusalem at the time of Christ and heard this news. Would you have run out to look into the tomb? Would you have believed and waited for his visit to you? Or would you have said, "Impossible!"?

Even the apostles did not believe the women's story. Peter and John ran to the tomb to see for themselves. They went back home amazed at what had happened.

That first Easter Day was confusing to the apostles. They talked, wondered, and questioned one another.

 While they were still speaking about this, Jesus stood in their midst and said to them, "Peace be with you." But they were startled and terrified and thought that they were seeing a ghost. Then he said to them, "Why are you troubled? And why do questions arise in your hearts? Look at my hands and my feet, that it is I myself. Touch me and see, because a ghost does not have flesh and bones as you can see I have." And as he said this, he showed them his hands and his feet. They were so glad and amazed that they could not believe it. He asked them, "Have you anything here to eat?" They gave him a piece of baked fish; he took it and ate it in front of them.

adapted from Luke 24:36–43

The apostles were filled with joy. They saw Jesus with their own eyes. He now had a glorified body and a new life. The apostles gathered around him as before. They touched him and spoke to him. He gave them new courage. They would wait for the Holy Spirit. Then they would praise the Lord and proclaim the Good News to the whole world: Jesus is glorious and will never die again.

On Easter we are filled with joy because Jesus is risen. He has destroyed sin and death. He lives and rules over the world and in us. His resurrection makes it possible for us to believe in him and to love him and others. It gives us new hope. We can look forward to living with Jesus forever in heaven.

Things to Do at Home

1. At Easter we see many signs of new life: the sun, rabbits, chicks, ducklings, eggs, and flowers. Discuss how these are signs of new life.

2. On Holy Saturday, take Easter food to a church where the priest blesses food. In union with our risen Lord, enjoy the food that also gives us life.

3. A candle's flame gives light. Jesus is the light and giver of new life. He takes away the darkness of sin and death. On Easter, set candles on the table.

4. In the Grace before Meals on Easter, ask the risen Jesus to keep your new life strong and add an "Alleluia."

We Remember

What do we celebrate on Easter?
On Easter we celebrate the resurrection of Jesus to new life and look forward to our resurrection.

We Respond

He is risen.
Alleluia!

We Review

Easter Hunt Find the correct word or phrase and write it on the line.

heaven   light   promises   risen   fire
Peace be with you   people   Holy Communion

1. In the Service of Light at the Easter Vigil the priest lights a new
   _____*fire*_____ .

2. The paschal candle shows that Jesus is our
   _____*light*_____ .

3. In the Liturgy of the Word we read about God's love for his
   _____*people*_____ .

4. In the Liturgy of Baptism we renew our baptismal
   _____*promises*_____ .

5. In the Liturgy of the Eucharist the newly baptized join us in offering the sacrifice of Jesus and in receiving him in
   _____*Holy Communion*_____ .

6. When the apostles were gathered together, Jesus appeared and said,
   "_____*Peace be with you*_____ ."

7. We are filled with joy on Easter because Jesus is
   _____*risen*_____ .

8. We hope to live with Jesus forever in
   _____*heaven*_____ .

We Are Mary's Children

"Hail Mary, Hail Mary, Hail Mary . . ." These words could be heard daily from the Cova da Iria near Fatima, Portugal, where Lucia took the family's sheep. Lucia's cousins, Jacinta and Francisco, came with her to watch the sheep. They joined her in praying the rosary each day and after lunch.

All three children loved Mary, but they also liked to sing, dance, and play. They shortened the rosary by saying only two words on each bead—Hail Mary, Our Father, or Glory Be!

One very hot summer morning it suddenly began to rain. The children went to a nearby cave to play, eat lunch, and say the rosary. As they said the last Hail Mary, the sun came out, and they went out to play. The children were startled by a strong wind that caused the pine trees to sway. The children looked to see what could be causing such a gust. They saw a brilliant light moving over the tops of the trees toward them. As it came closer, they saw a young man of fifteen. Lucia later described him as being as radiant as the sun shining through crystal.

"Don't be afraid," he said. "I am the Angel of Peace. Pray with me." He then knelt down, bowed until his forehead touched the ground, and prayed:

My God, I believe, I adore, I trust, and I love you! I beg pardon of you, and ask forgiveness for those who do not believe, do not adore, do not trust, and do not love you.

He repeated the prayer three times, and the children prayed with him. He told them to pray the prayer often. Then he disappeared. The children repeated the prayer like that until Francisco got tired.

A few weeks later the angel came again. The children were playing in a grove of fig trees behind Lucia's cottage. This time the angel told them to pray much, because Jesus and Mary had great plans for them. He told them to offer many prayers and sacrifices for sinners. Lucia asked how they were to sacrifice for sinners. The angel replied, "With all your power." He taught them another prayer and then left.

The children did what the angel had said. They made many sacrifices, such as

* giving their lunches to poor children,
* not taking a drink of water, even on the hottest days,
* giving up the songs and dances they loved so much, and
* accepting sufferings from their families and others.

These prayers and sacrifices helped the children to become more like Jesus. They also prepared the children to see Mary.

Our Lady appeared to the children the following year. She asked them to say the rosary every day for peace in the world. At one of her appearances, Our Lady showed the children a vision of hell. She asked them to pray and sacrifice much for sinners. She asked them to say this prayer after each decade of the rosary:

> O Jesus, forgive us our sins; save us from the fires of hell; lead all souls to heaven, especially those most in need of your mercy.

Our Lady told the children some things that would happen in the future. She asked that people stop sinning, which offends the Heart of Jesus and saddens her Immaculate Heart. Her children are those consecrated to her, those who love her and her Son.

To consecrate yourself to Mary is to offer yourself to her—not only in words but also in actions. It is to live as she would live and to do what she would do.

May is the month set aside for giving special honor to Mary. A good way to honor Mary is to consecrate yourself to her. There are many forms of the consecration. Here is one you might use.

Act of Consecration to Mary
My Queen, my Mother! I love you and give myself entirely to you. I give to you this day my eyes, my ears, my mouth, my heart, and my whole self. Since I am yours, keep me and guard me as your child forever.

Mary wants us to do the same things she asked the children at Fatima to do. Find some of these actions by filling in the missing words:

to pray and _sacrifice_ for sinners

to pray the _rosary_ for peace

to make up for offenses against _Jesus_

We honor Our Lady of Fatima on May 13. How will you honor Mary on this day? during her special month? for the rest of your life?

GLOSSARY

Pronunciation Key

a	h*a*llow	ie	l*ie*, sk*y*	uh	r*u*t, Asc*e*nsion, homi*l*y	kw	*qu*it, *qu*arrel
ah	f*a*ther	o	l*o*t			s	*s*tart, pre*ss*, *c*ent
aw	str*aw*, bef*o*re	oh	*ow*n, l*oa*n, l*o*ne	oo	s*oo*n, allel*u*ia	sh	A*s*cension, sta*ti*on
ay	m*ay*, tr*a*de	ow	c*ow*, h*ou*se	yoo	m*u*sic, b*eau*ty	th	*th*is, for*th*
e	p*e*t, f*ai*r, f*e*rret	oy	b*oy*, b*oi*l	g	*g*et	z	*z*oo, i*s*
ee	s*ee*n, sc*e*ne	u	f*u*ll, g*oo*d	j	*j*uice, e*dg*e	zh	mea*s*ure, vi*si*on
i	h*i*t			k	*k*itten, *c*at		

abortion (uh BOR shuhn): The act of deliberately destroying an unborn child. *Abortion* is a sin against the fifth commandment.

absolution (ab suh LOO shuhn): The forgiveness of sins spoken by the priest in the Sacrament of Reconciliation. The priest gives us *absolution* after we confess our sins and pray an Act of Contrition.

acclamation (ak kluh MAY shuhn): A short, enthusiastic response of praise at Mass. The *acclamation* following the Eucharistic Prayer is the Great Amen.

adultery (uh DUHL t[uh-]ree): The sin a married person commits when he or she gives to someone else the love promised to his or her marriage partner. The sixth commandment forbids *adultery*.

Advent: A period of four weeks of preparation for Christmas. *Advent* begins the Sunday on or closest to November 30.

alb (alb): A priest's long, white robe. An *alb* is worn under the chasuble during Mass.

alleluia (ah lay LOO yuh): An acclamation meaning "Praise God." At Mass we sing *alleluia* before reading the Gospel.

anoint (uh NOYNT): To put oil on things or people to show that power, strength, or healing is being given by God. Bishops *anoint* the hands of priests that they ordain.

Anointing of the Sick: The sacrament through which Jesus gives comfort, strength, and forgiveness to sick or injured people in danger of death and to the elderly. When people are seriously ill, they should ask for the *Anointing of the Sick*.

Ascension (uh SEN shuhn): The mystery of Jesus' return to the Father after he rose from the dead. We celebrate the feast of the *Ascension* forty days after Easter.

Assumption (uh SUHMP shuhn): Mary's privilege of being taken body and soul to heaven. We celebrate Mary's *Assumption* on August 15.

Baptism (BAP tiz uhm): The sacrament in which Jesus frees us from sin and gives us the grace by which we become God's children and members of the Church. After *Baptism* we can share in Christian worship.

Benediction (ben uh DIK shuhn): A blessing given by Jesus present in the Blessed Sacrament at the end of a eucharistic devotion. *Benediction* is part of the Eucharist, in which we adore, praise, and honor Jesus.

bishop (BISH uhp): A leader in the Church who has received full priestly powers as a successor of the apostles. The powers of a *bishop* include the authority to ordain and confirm, oversee other clergy, and care for all the people in a diocese.

canonized (CAN uhn iezd): Officially declared a saint by the Church. Not all holy people in heaven are *canonized*.

catechumen (kat uh KYOO muhn): A person in the Rite of Christian Initiation of Adults (RCIA) program who is preparing for Baptism. A *catechumen* learns about faith from the community.

celebrant (SEL uh bruhnt): The bishop, priest, or deacon who leads church services. The *celebrant* of the Mass must be an ordained priest or bishop.

chalice (CHAL uhs): The cup that holds the sacred wine. We may drink from the *chalice*.

chasuble (CHAZ[H] uh buhl): The outer vestment of the presider at Mass. The color of a *chasuble* is symbolic.

chrism (KRIZ uhm): A special oil used in Baptism, Confirmation, and Holy Orders. *Chrism* is blessed by the bishop on Holy Thursday or earlier in Holy Week.

ciborium (suh BOR ee uhm): The container that holds the sacred host. Communion is distributed from a *ciborium*.

Communion (kuhm YOON yuhn): The receiving of Jesus in the Holy Eucharist. We usually receive *Communion* during Mass.

concelebration (kon sel uh BRAY shuhn): The celebration of a Mass by two or more priests or bishops. The Mass for Confirmation is usually a *concelebration*.

Confirmation (kon fuhr MAY shuhn): The sacrament in which the Holy Spirit joins us more closely to Jesus and his Church and strengthens us as Christ's witnesses. The bishop is the usual minister of *Confirmation*.

conscience (KON shuhns): The power to judge what is the right or wrong thing to do. We must form a right *conscience* and obey it.

consecration (kon suh KRAY shuhn): The important moment of the Mass in which Jesus changes bread and wine into his own Body and Blood. The *consecration* takes place during the Eucharistic Prayer.

contrition (kuhn TRISH uhn): True sorrow for sin. We express our *contrition* before confessing our sins.

corporal (KAWR puhr uhl): A square, white cloth spread under the chalice, paten, and ciborium. A *corporal* is used under the Blessed Sacrament on the altar.

covenant (KUHV uh nuhnt): A solemn agreement. Marriage is a *covenant* between two people.

covet (KUHV uht): To want to take what belongs to someone else. The commandments tell us it is sinful to *covet*.

crosier (CROH zhuhr): A bishop's staff. The *crosier* is a symbol of a bishop's role as chief shepherd.

cruets (KROO its): The containers for the wine and water used in the Mass. The *cruets* are brought to the altar.

deacon (DEE kuhn): A man ordained by the bishop to proclaim God's Word, to assist in the liturgy, and to do works of charity. A *deacon* wears a stole over his left shoulder.

Easter: The Church's greatest day of celebration in honor of Jesus' resurrection. We sing the *Easter Alleluia* to praise God.

Eucharist (YOO k[uh-]rist): The sacrament of the Lord's Supper, which takes place at Mass when bread and wine are consecrated, offered to the Father, and received at Communion. It is the sacrament of the Lord's presence and of unity. Through the *Eucharist* we can celebrate and enter into the Paschal Mystery every day of the year except Good Friday.

eucharistic (yoo kuh RIS tik) **celebration** (sel uh BRAY shuhn): The Sacrifice of the Mass. The *eucharistic celebration* is our best means of worshiping God.

Eucharistic Prayer: The great prayer of the Mass during which bread and wine are changed into the Body and Blood of Jesus and offered to the Father. The *Eucharistic Prayer* gives praise and thanksgiving to God.

exposition (eks puh ZISH uhn): The time when the Blessed Sacrament in a monstrance or ciborium is honored on the altar. Some churches have *exposition* of the Blessed Sacrament all night on certain occasions.

G

grace: A gift by which we share in the life of God. Jesus offers us *grace* chiefly through prayer and the sacraments.

H

holiness: The quality of being godlike—filled with the Holy Spirit and love for God and his people. The highest goal of our lives is *holiness*.

Holy Orders: The sacrament in which a man is brought into an order of service to act in Christ's name in a special way as a deacon, priest, or bishop. Only a bishop may administer the Sacrament of *Holy Orders.*

Holy Week: The last week of Lent. *Holy Week* celebrates God's saving action through Christ's passion and resurrection.

homily (HOM uh lee): An explanation of the Scriptures by a priest or deacon. The *homily* proclaims how God has saved us from sin.

host (HOHST): The bread changed to the Body of Christ in the Eucharistic Prayer. The consecrated *host* is the Body of Christ.

I

Immaculate (i MAK yoo luht) **Conception** (kuhn SEP shuhn): The privilege that Mary had of being without sin from the first moment of her life. We celebrate the feast of the *Immaculate Conception* on December 8.

J

justice: Giving everyone what he or she deserves. The last seven commandments direct us to bring *justice* to all.

L

lectern (LEK tuhrn): A reading stand in churches from which Sacred Scriptures are read. The *lectern* is usually near the altar.

Lectionary (LEK shuh ner ee): The book containing the Bible readings for Mass. Sometimes the *Lectionary* is carried by the reader in the Entrance Procession.

Lent: Forty days of prayer and penance in preparation for Easter. During *Lent* people also prepare for Baptism.

liturgy (LIT uhr jee): The public worship of the Church. *Liturgy* includes the Mass, the sacraments, and the Liturgy of the Hours.

Liturgy of the Eucharist (YOO k[uh-]ruhst): The second main part of the Mass, in which Jesus becomes present, offers himself in sacrifice again, and comes to us in Communion. During the *Liturgy of the Eucharist,* bread and wine become the Body and Blood of Jesus.

Liturgy of the Hours: The official daily prayer of the Church. It contains psalms, readings, and intercessions. The *Liturgy of the Hours* is also called the Divine Office.

Liturgy of the Word: The first main part of the Mass, in which God's Word is proclaimed. God speaks to us during the *Liturgy of the Word.*

M

Marriage (MA rij) or **Matrimony** (MAT ruh moh nee): The sacrament in which a man and woman become husband and wife and promise to be faithful to each other. The Sacrament of *Marriage* or *Matrimony* binds a man and woman together for life.

minister (MIN uh stuhr): A person who assists in a special way in the Church. An ordained *minister* conducts worship, reads the Gospel, and administers the sacraments.

miter (MIE tuhr): The high, pointed hat of a bishop. The *miter* is removed when the celebrant prays.

monstrance (MON struhns): The metal holder used to expose the Blessed Sacrament. We adore the Sacred Host in the *monstrance.*

mortal (MAWR tuhl) **sin:** A serious offense that separates us from God completely and must be confessed. Anyone in *mortal sin* may not receive Holy Communion.

O

Ordination (ord uh NAY shuhn): The rite in which men become deacons, priests, or bishops. The bishop presides at an *ordination.*

original (uh RIJ uh nuhl) **sin:** 1. The first sin of Adam and Eve; 2. the sin with which all members of the human race are born. *Original sin* is removed by Baptism.

P

pall (PAWL): A small stiffly starched linen (or hemp) square, or sometimes a linen-covered cardboard, that is used to cover the chalice. A *pall* protects the wine.

paschal (PAS kuhl): Of or pertaining to the Jewish Passover or the Christian Easter. The Christian *paschal* season begins with Lent and ends at Pentecost.

Paschal Mystery (MIS tuhr ee): The passion, death, resurrection, and ascension of Jesus. We celebrate the *Paschal Mystery* at every sacrifice of the Mass.

paten (PAT uhn): A plate used at Mass to hold the bread or host. The priest lifts the chalice and *paten* during the Great Amen.

penance (PEN uhns): The prayers or good works offered to make up for sin and to help us change our lives. In the Sacrament of Reconciliation we are given a *penance*.

Penitential (pen uh TEN chuhl) **Rite** (RIET): That part of the Mass before the Liturgy of the Word in which we ask God's forgiveness for our sins. The *Penitential Rite* prepares us to celebrate the Eucharist.

Pentecost (PENT i kawst): The day Jesus sent the Holy Spirit to the Church. We celebrate *Pentecost* fifty days after Easter Sunday.

Preface (PREF uhs): The prayer of thanksgiving that begins the Eucharistic Prayer of the Mass. The *Preface* tells us of God's great love.

priest (PREEST): A man called by God to strengthen Christian community and worship. Every *priest* is ordained by a bishop to act in the name of Christ.

proclaim (pro KLAYM): To announce a message. Priests and deacons *proclaim* the Word of God during Mass.

pure (PYOOR): Without sin; free from anything displeasing to God. God commands us to be *pure* in our thoughts, words, desires, and actions.

purificator (PYOOR uh fuh kay tuhr): A white cloth used to dry the priest's fingers, the chalice, and paten. A *purificator* sometimes has a small red cross embroidered at its center.

purity (PYOOR uh tee): Freedom from guilt or sin, especially in the matters of sex. We protect our *purity* through self-control.

R

reconcile (REK uhn siel): To make peace. We *reconcile* differences we have with others.

Reconciliation (rek uhn sil ee AY shuhn), **Sacrament** (SAK ruh muhnt) **of:** The sacrament, also known as Penance, in which we confess our sins to a priest and make peace with God and others. Jesus forgives our sins in the *Sacrament of Reconciliation*.

relic (REL ik): A part of a saint's body or anything the saint used or touched. We show reverence for a *relic*.

religious (ri LIJ uhs): Priests, brothers, and sisters, who dedicate their lives to God through vows and who usually live in community. *Religious* are called to serve the Church in many ways.

restitution (res tuh T[Y]OO shuhn): The act of making up for the loss of or damage to another's property. *Restitution* must be made whenever anything is damaged or stolen.

Resurrection (rez uhr REK shuhn): Jesus' rising from the dead on the third day after he was buried. We celebrate the *Resurrection* of Jesus on Easter.

rite (RIET): The words and actions of a religious service or sacrament. Faith in Jesus is expressed in the *rite* of Baptism.

Rite of Christian (KRIS[H] chuhn) **Initiation** (in ish ee AY shuhn) **of Adults** (uh DUHLTS) **(RCIA):** A program by which adults learn to live the Catholic faith and are initiated into the Church. Catechumens in the *Rite of Christian Initiation of Adults (RCIA)* program are preparing for Baptism.

S

sacrament (SAK ruh muhnt): A sacred sign in which we meet Jesus and receive from him a share in God's life. Every *sacrament* is a celebration.

sacramental (sak ruh MEN tuhl): Words, actions, or objects blessed by the Church that bring us closer to God. A blessed palm branch is a *sacramental*.

Sacramentary (sak ruh MEN tuh ree): The book that contains the prayers used for the celebration of the Eucharist. The *Sacramentary* is usually on the altar for the celebrant to use during Mass.

sacred (SAY kruhd): Holy; set apart for the service of God. A church is a *sacred* place.

sacrifice (SAK ruh fies): A gift offered to God as an act of worship. The Mass is our greatest *sacrifice*.

sin: An offense against God and others. We commit a *sin* when we choose to do what we know is wrong.

sponsor (SPON suhr): A person who helps the one being confirmed to know and practice the faith. A *sponsor* should be a good Christian.

stole (STOHL): A long, narrow vestment worn around the neck and over the shoulders. A *stole* is a symbol of the powers of the priesthood.

suicide (SOO uh sied): The act of deliberately and intentionally taking one's own life. *Suicide* is a sin against the fifth commandment.

synagogue (SIN uh gog): A building or place of public worship for Jewish people. Jesus worshiped in a *synagogue*.

V

venial (VEE nyuhl) **sin:** Any thought, word, action, or omission that offends God in a less serious way than mortal sin. *Venial sin* weakens our friendship with God and the Church.

Viaticum (vie AT i kuhm): The rite of Holy Communion received by someone who is dying. *Viaticum* gives the dying strength for their journey through death.

vocation (voh KAY shuhn): A call from God to live a special way of life. A priest becomes holy in his *vocation*.

vows: Promises made to God to do something that is good and pleasing to him. Usually, religious make three *vows*.

W

witness (WIT nuhs): A person who affirms by word or example his or her faith. Each of us is a *witness* to Jesus when we show his love to others.

worship (WUHR ship): The honor and praise we give to God. We give God *worship* through prayer and service and especially in the celebration of the Eucharist.

Y

Yahweh (YAH way): The name God used to identify himself to Moses. The meaning of *Yahweh* is "I Am Who Am."

synagogue (SIN uh gog): A building or place of public worship for Jewish people. Jesus worshiped in a *synagogue*.

I

Ignatius of Loyola, St., 74–75
Incense, 32
Initiation, sacraments of, 11, 16, 20, 28, 42, 113. *See also* Sacraments: Baptism; Confirmation; Eucharist
Isaac Jogues, St., 75
Isaiah, 96
Israelites (chosen people), 3, 28, 35

J

Jacinta of Fatima, 168, 193–94
Jairus, 102
James, St., 165, 188
Jerome, St., 61
Jerusalem, 21, 187, 191
Jesuit Volunteers, 25
Jesuits, 74, 131
Jesus
  divinity of, 58
  friendship with, 15, 18, 28, 52, 58, 65, 72, 84
  fullness of revelation of, 54–55, 72
  as healer, 10, 143
  holiness of, 112
  as judge of the living and the dead, 171–72, 176–77, 183, 185
  love of, for his Father, 8, 9, 11, 66, 112
  miracles of
    cure of Jairus' daughter, 102–3
    multiplication of the loaves and fish, 28, 34, 73
  obedience of, 10, 84
  parables of
    Foolish Rich Farmer, 157
    Good Shepherd, 143
    Last Judgment, 171–72, 176–77
    Lazarus and the Rich Man, 158
    Mystery of a Dying Seed, 186
  passion and death of, 8, 10, 28, 84, 143, 186–87, 188–89
  as priest, 9–10, 129, 137
  relation of, to Father and Spirit, 8–9, 21–22, 58, 71, 84
  resurrection of, 8, 28, 186, 190–92
  sacrifice of, 8, 28, 59, 64, 84, 186–90
  as Savior, 9, 11, 17, 28, 36, 44, 58–59, 61, 71, 84, 143, 183
  as Word of God, 29, 52–53, 54, 55
Jewish people, 3, 10, 87
Joachim, St., 184
John the Baptist, 184–85
John, St., the Evangelist, 9, 188, 189, 191

John Neumann, St., 69
John Paul II, 62
Jordan River, 184–85
Joseph, St., 33
Judas, 188
Judgment after death, 171–72, 176–77
Justice, 158, 162

K

Keys to the Kingdom, 95
Kids for Saving Earth™, 148–49
Kindness, 165, 166
Kneeling, 6

L

Last Judgment. *See* Jesus, parables of
Last Supper, 21, 28–29, 35, 59, 60, 63, 71, 78, 187
Lathrop, Rose Hawthorne, 100–101
Law, Church, 16, 25, 29, 45, 90
Lawrence, St., 159–60
Lay ministries, 24, 32, 97, 116, 129, 134
Laying on of hands, 11, 21, 22, 23, 99, 102, 103, 128–29, 132–34, 139
Lazarus and the Rich Man. *See* Jesus, parables of
Lectionary, 54, 57
Lent, 45, 186–89
Lepers, 26
Letters. *See* Epistles
Lies, 92, 163–64, 168
Life, sacredness of, 142–48, 153, 157, 158
Liturgy, 12, 13, 14, 41, 54, 132, 187
Liturgy of the Eucharist. *See* Sacraments, Eucharist
Liturgy of the Hours, 5, 12, 13, 129
Liturgy of the Word, 47, 52–56, 60, 77, 79, 80, 121, 190, 192
Lord's Day, 44. *See also* Sunday
Lord's Prayer. *See* Prayer(s), Our Father
Louis, St., 5
Love
  children as living reminders of, 124–27
  commandments of, for others, 150–55, 175
  God's, given in sacraments, 12, 29, 42, 90, 121–27, 140
  healing nature of, 86, 87–92, 96, 109
  living united in God's, 18, 66, 94, 150, 165, 175, 186
  words that express, 165
Lucia of Fatima, 168, 193–94
Luke, St., 9

M

Manna, 28
Mark, St., 9
Marriage. *See* Sacraments
Martin de Porres, St., 173
Martyr, 26, 159–60
Mary, the Blessed Mother, 21, 45, 51
  Act of Consecration to, 194
  Hail (Ave Maria). *See* Prayer(s)
  as intercessor for Christians, 151, 152
  as Mother of Jesus, 33, 62, 184
  as Our Lady of Fatima, 168, 193–94
  as our model in making choices, 83, 135, 151, 152, 184, 185, 194
  as our mother, 151, 189, 194
Maryknoll Lay Missions, 25
Mass (Eucharistic Liturgy), 10, 48, 129, 152
  celebrated year-long with different themes, 45
  celebration of sacraments during, 22, 28, 44, 58–61, 98, 121
  living the, 76
  of the Lord's Supper, 187
  order of, outlined, 47, 79
  parts of, described, 48–49, 52–55, 58–61, 65, 67–68, 71–73
  as perfect thanksgiving, 44, 48, 58–61, 63
  on Sunday and holy days, 6, 45
  as unity with God, 28–29, 44, 59–61, 63, 64, 65–68, 70, 73
Matrimony. *See* Sacraments
Matthew, St., 9
Maximilian Kolbe, St., 62
Memorial acclamation, 61
Miracles. *See* Jesus, miracles of
Missionaries, 3, 24–25, 72–75, 76, 131, 144
Missionaries of Charity, 144
Mission work, 24–25, 72–75, 129–31
Miter, 133, 134
Monstrance, 32, 33, 40
Mortal sin. *See* Sin
Moses, 158
Mother Marianne of Molokai, 26
Mother Teresa of Calcutta, 144, 145
Mysteries, 11, 45, 80, 96
Mystery of a Dying Seed. *See* Jesus, parables of

N

Nazareth, 184
New commandment, 187
New Covenant, 187

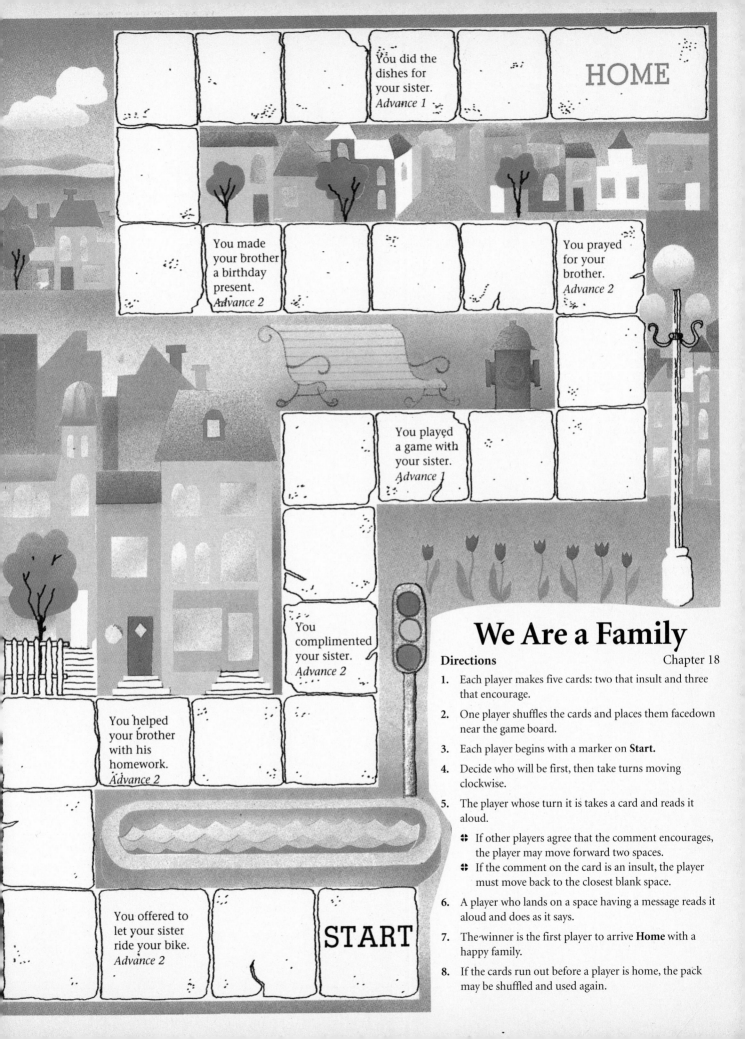

You did the dishes for your sister. *Advance 1*

HOME

You made your brother a birthday present. *Advance 2*

You prayed for your brother. *Advance 2*

You played a game with your sister. *Advance 1*

You complimented your sister. *Advance 2*

You helped your brother with his homework. *Advance 2*

You offered to let your sister ride your bike. *Advance 2*

START

We Are a Family

Directions   Chapter 18

1. Each player makes five cards: two that insult and three that encourage.

2. One player shuffles the cards and places them facedown near the game board.

3. Each player begins with a marker on **Start**.

4. Decide who will be first, then take turns moving clockwise.

5. The player whose turn it is takes a card and reads it aloud.
    ✜ If other players agree that the comment encourages, the player may move forward two spaces.
    ✜ If the comment on the card is an insult, the player must move back to the closest blank space.

6. A player who lands on a space having a message reads it aloud and does as it says.

7. The winner is the first player to arrive **Home** with a happy family.

8. If the cards run out before a player is home, the pack may be shuffled and used again.

A Prayer for My Parents

Lord, stretch out your hand and bless my father and mother.

Grant that they may share with each other the gifts of your love, and become one in heart and mind. May they witness to you in their marriage.

Give your blessings to my mother.
May she be a faithful wife and a good mother, helping us to grow in love.

Give your blessings to my father.
May he always be a faithful husband and a good father, showing us how to live in your love.

Lord, grant that my parents, who come together at your table on Earth, may one day share the joy of your feast in heaven.

adapted from *Nuptial Blessing*

Daily Offering

O Jesus, through the Immaculate Heart of Mary, I offer you my prayers, works, joys, and sufferings of this day in union with the Holy Sacrifice of the Mass throughout the world. I offer them for all the intentions of your Sacred Heart: the salvation of souls, reparation for sin, the reunion of all Christians. I offer them for the intentions of our bishops and of all Apostles of Prayer, and in particular for those recommended by our Holy Father this month.

You have put on Christ. You have been baptized in him.

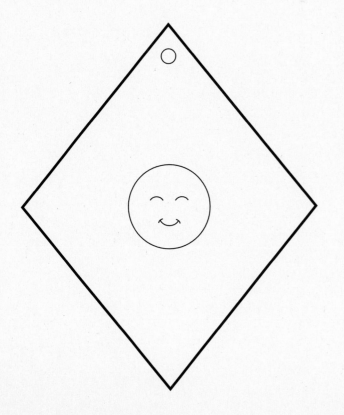

Take my life and let it be
consecrated, Lord, to thee.

Take my hands and let them move
at the impulse of thy love.

Take my feet and let them be
swift and beautiful for thee.

Take my voice and let it sing
always, only for my king.

Take my lips and let them be
filled with messages from thee.

Take my moments and my days.
Let them flow in ceaseless praise.

Take my intellect and use
every power as thou shall choose.

Take my heart: it is thine own.
Let it be thy royal throne.

Take my love, O Lord! I pour
at thy feet its treasure store.

Take myself and I will be
ever, only, all for thee! Amen.

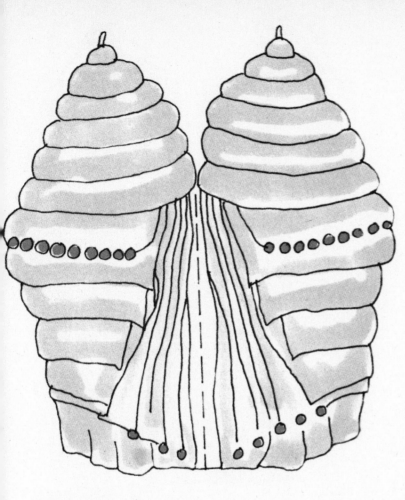

To Make the Chrysalis

1. Cut out the chrysalis.
2. Fold it in half on the dotted line.
3. Tape the edge closed but leave the top open.
4. Print your name on the chrysalis.
5. Punch a hole near the top of the chrysalis. Insert a piece of yarn.
6. Tie the yarn to form a hanger.

To Make a Butterfly

1. Cut out the butterfly.
2. Print your Lenten resolution on the blank side.
3. Carefully fold the butterfly in half. Then fold it in half again.
4. Gently roll the folded butterfly into a cylinder shape. Place it in the chrysalis.
5. Hang the chrysalis on a tree branch.
6. Once each week, take your butterfly out. Read your resolution. If you have kept it, color one part of the butterfly. By Easter the entire butterfly should be colored!

Lent Is a Time for Reconciliation

Catechist: Today we gather together to think about how God loves us. He calls us to follow Jesus more closely. We have sinned, and we need forgiveness. Together we will prepare for the Sacrament of Reconciliation.

Leader: In the Sacrament of Reconciliation, Jesus wants to give us a new heart and a new spirit. He wants us to love and serve God and one another as he did. Jesus loves us so much! He knows we have sinned against God and have hurt ourselves and others, but he still loves us. Let us listen to a Scripture reading. It tells us how God promised his people he would forgive their sins and change their hearts.

Reader: A reading from the prophet Ezekiel.

The nations shall know that I am the LORD . . . when I prove my holiness through you. For I will take you away from among the nations, gather you from all the foreign lands, and bring you back to your own land. I will sprinkle clean water upon you to cleanse you from all your sins. . . . I will give you a new heart and a new spirit, taking from your bodies your stony hearts and giving you natural hearts. I will put my spirit within you and make you keep my commandments. . . . You will be my people and I will be your God.

adapted from Ezekiel 36:23–28

All: Thanks be to God. Lord, give us a new heart and a new spirit.

A Psalm in Praise of God's Service

Boys: Bless the LORD, O my soul,
And remember all his kindnesses.

Girls: He forgives all our sins
And heals all our ills.

All: He saves us from all danger
And loves us tenderly.

Boys: He fills our life with good things
And gives us strength and courage.

Girls: The LORD is merciful and loving.
He does not punish us
As our guilt and sins deserve.

Boys: For as high as the heavens are above
the earth,
So great is his kindness toward those
who love him.

Girls: As far as the east is from the west,
So far does he put our sins from us.

All: As a father is kind to his children
So the LORD is kind to those who
love him.
Bless the LORD, O my soul!

adapted from Psalm 103

Leader: Let us ask the Holy Spirit to help us prepare to confess our sins.

All: Come, Holy Spirit, give light to our minds. Help us to know our sins and be truly sorry for them. Give us the courage to admit them and to be more faithful in Christ's love.

Catechist: Let us think of how we have offended God and hurt ourselves and others by our sins. What have we done at home, in school, in other places?

Jesus said, "You shall love the Lord your God with all your heart, with all your soul, with all your mind, and with all your strength" (Mark 12:30).

Do you really love God above all things?

Do you take time each day to pray to him?

Have you always used his name with respect?

Have you celebrated every Sunday and holy day with Mass?

Do you thank God each day for his goodness to you?

Jesus said, *"You shall love your neighbor as yourself"* (Mark 12:31).

Have you always obeyed your parents, teachers, and those in authority—or did you answer back or show disrespect in other ways?

Have you been kind to everyone? Or did you fight, argue, call people names, or do other mean things?

Have you been faithful to your promises?

Have you always controlled your anger—or have you hurt yourself or others by what you said or did when you were angry?

Have you asked the people you've hurt to forgive you?

Have you always respected your own body and the bodies of others as God's gifts—or have you said or done things that do not honor the human body as a temple of God?

Have you been honest—or have you cheated in schoolwork or in games?

Have you been faithful in doing your duties—or have you been lazy and not done them?

Have you respected what belongs to others—or have you taken or damaged something that did not belong to you?

Have you taken good care of your belongings? Have you shared with others?

Have the things you said about others always been kind and true—or have you talked about others unkindly?

Have you always told the truth?

Have you done or failed to do anything else for which you are sorry?

Leader: Let us tell God we are sorry.

All: My God, I am sorry for my sins with
    all my heart.
In choosing to do wrong
and failing to do good,
I have sinned against you
whom I should love above all things.
I firmly intend, with your help,
to do penance,
to sin no more,
and to avoid whatever leads me to sin.
Our Savior Jesus Christ
suffered and died for us.
In his name, my God, have mercy.
Rite of Reconciliation

Leader: Father of mercy and love,
you do not wish sinners to die
but to turn back to you and live.
Help us turn from our sins
and live for you alone.
May we confess our sins,
receive your forgiveness,
and always be grateful for your
    loving kindness.
Help us to live the truth in love
and grow into the fullness of Christ,
    your Son,
who lives and reigns for ever and ever.
Amen.
adapted from *Rite of Reconciliation*

Let us give the sign of peace to each other and close with a song.

- Have I tried to take care of my belongings? Have I been careful not to waste God's gifts so that others can enjoy them too? Have I shared with others?
- Have I taken anything that is not mine? Have I returned what I borrowed? Have I damaged anything that belonged to someone else? If so, have I paid for or repaired the damage?
- Have I always spoken the truth? Have I spoken kindly about others? Have I kept secrets and promises?
- Have I chosen good friends? Have I been faithful to them?
- Am I bothered by anything else I did wrong?
- Do I want to talk to the priest about something in confession?

I Think of God's Forgiving Love

You have been told . . . what is good,
 and what the LORD requires of you:
Only to do the right and to love goodness,
 and to walk humbly with your God.

But as for me, I will look to the LORD,
 I will put my trust in God my savior;
 my God will hear me!

Micah 6:8; 7:7

Happy is the person whose fault is
 taken away,
 whose sin is covered.
I admitted to you that I had sinned,
 I did not hide my faults. . . .
 and you took away the guilt of
 my sin.
Be glad in the LORD and rejoice, you just;
 exult, all you upright of heart.

adapted from Psalm 32:1, 5, 11

I Confess My Sins to the Priest

- The priest welcomes me, and I greet him.
- I make the Sign of the Cross.
- The priest says a prayer to help me remember God's forgiving love.
- I say, "Amen."
- Either the priest or I may read God's Word from the Bible.
- I make my confession.
- When I am finished telling the priest my sins, I say, "I am sorry for all my sins."
- The priest gives me a penance. I listen to what he says. Then I tell God I am sorry.
- As he absolves me, I make the Sign of the Cross and then say, "Amen."
- The priest says, "Give thanks to the Lord for he is good."
- I say, "His mercy endures forever."

I Do My Penance

My Reconciliation Booklet

How numerous have you made,
 O LORD, my God, your wondrous deeds!
And in your plans for us
 there is none to equal you;
Should I wish to declare or to tell them,
 they would be too many to recount.

Psalm 40:6

Name _____

I Examine My Conscience

Have I Loved God?

✤ Have I spent some time praying to God each day? in the morning? at night? Did I try to give God my full attention when I prayed?

✤ Have I always used God's name with love and respect?

✤ Have I participated in Mass every Sunday and holy day? If I missed Mass, was it for an important reason or only because I did not want to go? Have I really tried to pray and sing at Mass? Have I been on time?

✤ Have I thanked God for all his goodness to me?

✤ Have I told God that I was sorry when I sinned?

✤ Have I often asked God to help me?

Have I Loved Myself and Others?

✤ Have I been obedient and respectful to my parents and others who care for me? When I have been a leader, have I tried to do what I thought was best for everyone?

✤ Have I taken care of the gift of my life and that of others? Have I avoided drugs and other things that would harm my health? Have I hurt anyone by fighting? by jokes? by calling names? by mean words? Have I been unkind to people who were poor or different from me?

✤ Have I asked forgiveness when I hurt someone? Have I used my gifts of mind and body to bring joy to others?

✤ Have I shown respect for my body? for others' bodies? Have I told or listened to stories that make fun of the human body? Have I treated my own body or another's in the wrong way? Have I looked at pictures that do not respect God's gift of sex?

God loves us and asks us to love him, ourselves, and others. When we turn from God and fail to love, Jesus invites us to return to him so that he can forgive us. He has given us his Holy Spirit to help us. Let us now prepare to meet Jesus in the Sacrament of Reconciliation.

I Pray to the Holy Spirit

Come, Holy Spirit, and help me to know how much God loves me and wants to forgive me. Help me to see and to love the goodness God has placed in me and in others. You have asked me to love God, myself, and others. Show me how I have failed and help me to be sorry for my sins.

Come, Holy Spirit,
  fill the hearts of your faithful
And kindle in them
  the fire of your love.

I Pray an Act of Contrition

My God,
I am sorry for my sins with all my heart.
In choosing to do wrong
and failing to do good,
I have sinned against you
whom I should love above all things.
I firmly intend, with your help,
to do penance,
to sin no more,
and to avoid whatever leads me to sin.
Our Savior Jesus Christ
suffered and died for us.
In his name, my God, have mercy.

Celebrating the Eucharist

Supplication ✙ Adoration ✙ Contrition ✙ Thanksgiving

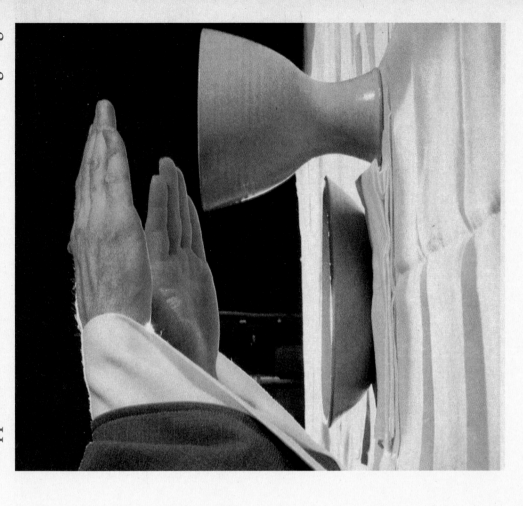

Blessing

Priest: May God bless you, the Father, and the Son, ✝ and the Holy Spirit.

All: Amen.

Dismissal

(The deacon or the priest then sends us forth and we respond:)

All: Thanks be to God.

Jesus goes with you to help you take his love into the world. How will you show his love?

Thanksgiving after Communion

(Use the letters in the word ALTAR to help you talk with Jesus.)

Adore God, telling him how great and wonderful he is. Name one thing you will do today to give him praise and honor.

Love God, telling him about your happy and sad times. Express your appreciation for his love for you. Ask him how he wants you to show his love to others.

Thank God for all his goodness. Mention some special things you are thankful for. Thank God for the gift of the Eucharist, and tell him what your gift to him will be today.

Ask God to help you, your family, and all people. Say exactly how you need God's help; what your family and others need to come closer to him. Ask to be the best person you can be.

Resolve to do something special to show God you love him. What do you need to do or avoid in order to become more like God? Make that your resolution, and ask God to help you keep it.

"Do this in memory of me."
Luke 22:19

Name _____

12

Prayer before Mass

Heavenly Father, we celebrate this Mass to show our faith and love as a community. We praise and thank you for your great goodness. We ask you to free us from sin and give us all we need to grow closer to you and to your people.

We unite and offer ourselves with Jesus, your Son, in reparation for sin, for the spread of the kingdom, for our special intentions [name them], and for all other intentions pleasing to you.

May we leave this celebration filled with new love and generosity to serve you and others. We ask this through Jesus your Son and through the Holy Spirit. Amen.

+ +

Note: This booklet contains the **Order of the Mass.** These prayers stay the same throughout the year. The prayers and readings that change daily according to the feasts or time of the Church year can be found in a Sunday or daily missal or missalette.

+ +

Breaking of the Bread

(*We pray to prepare for Christ's coming to our hearts.*)

All: Lamb of God, you take away the sins of the world:
have mercy on us.
Lamb of God, you take away the sins of the world:
have mercy on us.
Lamb of God, you take away the sins of the world:
grant us peace.

Communion

Priest: This is the Lamb of God
who takes away the sins of the world.
Happy are those who are called to his supper.

All: Lord, I am not worthy to receive you,
but only say the word and I shall be healed.

(*The priest receives Communion. Then we receive Jesus' Body and Blood from the priest or another minister.*)

Period of Silence or Song of Praise

[*See page 12 for thanksgiving ideas.*]

Prayer after Communion (*From the Mass of the day*)

Priest: Let us pray . . . through Christ our Lord.
All: Amen.

Concluding Rite

Greeting

Priest: The Lord be with you.
All: And also with you.

Introductory Rites

Entrance Procession

(*A song may be sung.*)

Greeting

Priest: In the name of the Father, and of the Son, and of the Holy Spirit.

All: Amen.

(*The priest greets the people and we respond:*)

All: And also with you.

Penitential Rite

(*The priest asks us to call to mind our sins. We respond with either "Lord, have mercy" or the following prayer:*)

All: I confess to almighty God,
and to you, my brothers and sisters,
that I have sinned through my own fault
in my thoughts and in my words,
in what I have done,
and in what I have failed to do;
and I ask blessed Mary, ever virgin,
all the angels and saints,
and you, my brothers and sisters,
to pray for me to the Lord our God.

Priest: May almighty God have mercy on us,
forgive us our sins,
and bring us to everlasting life.

All: Amen.

Communion Rite

The Lord's Prayer

Priest: Let us pray with confidence to the Father in the words our Savior gave us.

All: Our Father . . .

Priest: Deliver us, Lord, from every evil,
and grant us peace in our day.
In your mercy keep us free from sin
and protect us from all anxiety
as we wait in joyful hope
for the coming of our Savior, Jesus Christ.

All: For the kingdom, the power and the glory are yours, now and forever.

Sign of Peace

Priest: Lord Jesus Christ, you said to your apostles:
I leave you peace, my peace I give you.
Look not on our sins, but on the faith of your Church, and grant us the peace and unity of your kingdom where you live forever and ever.

All: Amen.

Priest: The peace of the Lord be with you always.

All: And also with you.

Priest: Let us offer each other a sign of peace.

(*We wish one another the peace of Christ.*)

In your heart tell Jesus you will try to live in peace with others today.

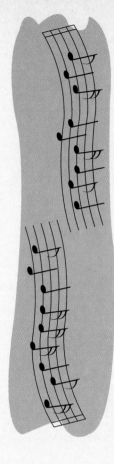

Glory to God (*Said or sung on Sundays and special feasts*)

Let your voice show joy and love as you praise God.

All: Glory to God in the highest,
and peace to his people on earth.

Lord, God, heavenly King,
almighty God and Father,
we worship you, we give you thanks,
we praise you for your glory.

Lord Jesus Christ, only Son of the Father,
Lord God, Lamb of God,
you take away the sins of the world:
have mercy on us;
you are seated at the right hand of the Father:
receive our prayer.

For you alone are the Holy One,
you alone are the Lord,
you alone are the Most High,
Jesus Christ,
with the Holy Spirit,
in the glory of God the Father.
Amen.

Opening Prayer

Priest: Let us pray . . . (*From the Mass of the day*)
All: Amen. (*Meaning So be it, Lord. This is my prayer also!*)

Priest: (*Continues with the Eucharistic Prayer, which includes the Narrative of the Last Supper*)

Take this, all of you, and eat it:
this is my body which will be given up for you.

Take this, all of you, and drink from it:
this is the cup of my blood,
the blood of the new and everlasting covenant.
It will be shed for you and for all
so that sins may be forgiven.
Do this in memory of me.

Let us proclaim the mystery of faith:

All: (*We pray one of the following:*)
✠ Christ has died,
Christ is risen,
Christ will come again.

✠ Dying you destroyed our death,
rising you restored our life.
Lord Jesus, come in glory.

✠ When we eat this bread and drink this cup,
we proclaim your death, Lord Jesus,
until you come in glory.

✠ Lord, by your cross and resurrection
you have set us free.
You are the Savior of the world.

Priest: (*Continues by recalling Christ's death and resurrection, prays for the coming of the Holy Spirit, and remembers the saints, the living, and the dead. He concludes:*)

Priest: Through him, with him, in him, in the unity of the Holy Spirit, all glory and honor is yours, almighty Father, for ever and ever.

All: Amen! (*We make the Eucharistic Prayer ours by this response.*)

Liturgy of the Word

First Reading

(All readings are from the Mass of the day.)

Reader: *(At the end)* The Word of the Lord.

    All: Thanks be to God.

Responsorial Psalm

(We pray the response to the psalm verses.)

Second Reading *(On Sundays and special feasts)*

Reader: *(At the end)* The Word of the Lord.

    All: Thanks be to God.

Gospel Acclamation *(Alleluia or Lenten verse)*

Gospel

Deacon (Priest): A reading from the holy Gospel according to . . .

    All: Glory to you, Lord.

Deacon (Priest): *(At the end)* The Gospel of the Lord.

    All: Praise to you, Lord Jesus Christ.

Homily

What is God telling you today?

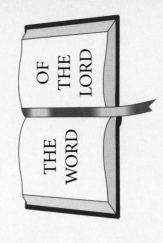

Prayer Over the Gifts *(From the Mass of the day)*

Priest: Let us pray . . . through Christ our Lord.

    All: Amen.

Eucharistic Prayer

(The priest invites us to prepare to offer Jesus' gift.)

Priest: The Lord be with you.

    All: And also with you.

Priest: Lift up your hearts.

    All: We lift them up to the Lord.

Priest: Let us give thanks to the Lord our God.

    All: It is right to give him thanks and praise.

Priest: Father, all-powerful and ever-living God . . .

(The priest then prays one of the Eucharistic Prayers. In each prayer he tells why it is good to praise God.)

For what do I want to thank God?

(We sing or pray with all the angels and saints.)

    All: Holy, holy, holy Lord, God of power and might, heaven and earth are full of your glory. Hosanna in the highest. Blessed is he who comes in the name of the Lord. Hosanna in the highest.

Profession of Faith (*On Sundays and special feasts*)

Priest: We believe in one God,

All: the Father, the Almighty,
maker of heaven and earth,
of all that is seen and unseen.

We believe in one Lord Jesus Christ,
the only Son of God,
eternally begotten of the Father,
God from God, Light from Light,
true God from true God,
begotten, not made, one in Being with the Father.
Through him all things were made.
For us men and for our salvation
he came down from heaven:

(We bow during the next two lines.)
by the power of the Holy Spirit
he was born of the Virgin Mary, and became man.

For our sake he was crucified under Pontius Pilate;
he suffered, died, and was buried.
On the third day he rose again
in fulfillment of the Scriptures;
he ascended into heaven
and is seated at the right hand of the Father.

He will come again in glory to judge the living and
the dead,
and his kingdom will have no end.

We believe in the Holy Spirit, the Lord, the giver
of life,
who proceeds from the Father and the Son.
With the Father and the Son he is worshiped
and glorified.

6

He has spoken through the Prophets.
We believe in one holy catholic and apostolic
Church.
We acknowledge one baptism for the forgiveness
of sins.
We look for the resurrection of the dead,
and the life of the world to come. Amen.

General Intercessions

(In these prayers we pray to God for the Church, the world, and for those in need.)

Today I especially pray for . . .

Liturgy of the Eucharist

Preparation of the Altar and Gifts

(As the bread and wine are brought to altar, we sing a hymn. If the priest says aloud the prayers blessing God for bread and wine, we respond to them:)

All: Blessed be God forever.

(The priest washes his hands.)

Invitation to Prayer over the Gifts

Priest: Pray, my brothers and sisters, that our sacrifice
may be acceptable to God, the almighty Father.

All: May the Lord accept the sacrifice at your hands
for the praise and glory of his name,
for our good and the good of all his Church.

7

Life with Christ

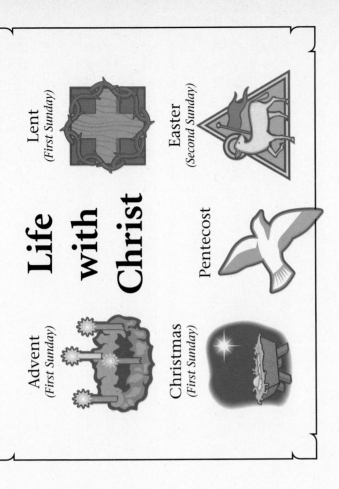

Advent
(First Sunday)

Lent
(First Sunday)

Christmas
(First Sunday)

Easter
(Second Sunday)

Pentecost

Dear Friend of Jesus,

This booklet can help you prepare for the liturgies listed, increase your knowledge of Sacred Scripture, and help you pray. Scripture, liturgy, and prayer are all important in your relationship with Jesus.

For each liturgy, use a Bible, a Sunday missal, or a missalette. Read the Scripture references and answer the questions for the current year. Your teacher will tell you whether this is year A, B, or C. Think about the Word of God you have read. Close with prayer, using the ideas at the end of the section.

May God the Father, the Son, and the Holy Spirit bless you as you learn more about God's goodness and love.

Name _____

Sequence *(Prose form or poetic form)*

1. What names for the Holy Spirit are used in this prayer? _____

2. The last paragraph (prose) or the last two verses (poem) are a good prayer. Who is included in the "faithful"? _____

Gospel *[A, B, C] Jn 20:19–23*

1. Jesus gives the Holy Spirit to his apostles. What power does the Spirit give them?

2. How does the Holy Spirit help us through this power?

✝ Like the apostles, you received the Holy Spirit at Baptism. You received gifts that enable you to know and do God's will and to become more like Jesus. Ask the Holy Spirit to renew his gifts in you that you may be the best person you can possibly be—a Christlike person!

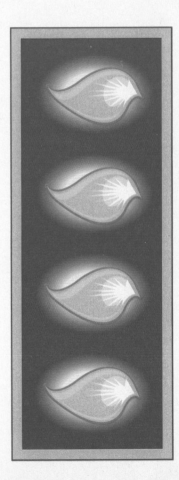

First Sunday of Advent
First Reading

[A] *Is 2:1–5*

1. What will the Lord do for us if we climb his mountain?
2. What does it mean to "walk in his [the Lord's] paths"?

[B] *Is 63:16–17, 19; 64:2–7*

1. Why is the prophet asking the Lord to return?
2. Isaiah calls us the clay and God the potter. What is the relationship between the potter and the clay?

[C] *Jer 33:14–16*

1. Who is the "just shoot"? What will the "shoot" do?
2. In what situations can you do what is right and just?

Responsorial Psalm

[A] *Ps 122:1–9*

1. How many references to peace are in this psalm?
2. How can you bring peace to others this week?

[B] *Ps 80:2–3, 15–16, 18–19*

1. What do we ask the Shepherd of Israel to do for us?
2. We ask the Lord to save us and give us new life. What does this mean to you?

[C] *Ps 25:4–5, 8–10, 14*

1. What do we ask God to teach us?
2. What does having the friendship of God mean to you?

✝ Talk to our Risen Lord. Thank him for his victory over death! Tell him how you will show by your words and actions, especially this week, that you believe in him and are his follower. We hear many Alleluias this season. Think what it means to be an "alleluia person." Can you be one?

Pentecost
First Reading [A, B, C] *Acts 2:1–11*

1. What were the apostles able to do after they received the Holy Spirit?
2. How does the Spirit speak to us?

Responsorial Psalm [A, B, C] *Ps 104:1, 24, 29–31, 34*

1. Why do we ask God to send his Spirit?
2. How can you show God that you appreciate his beautiful creation?

Second Reading [A, B, C] *1 Cor 12:3–7, 12–13*

1. What can we say through the power of the Holy Spirit?
2. To what does Paul compare us in order to show that we are united yet different?

Second Reading

[A] Rom 13:11–14

1. Why does Paul tell us to wake from sleep?
2. How can you "put on the Lord Jesus Christ"?

[B] 1 Cor 1:3–9

1. What is it that Christ will do for us?
2. God is faithful to you. How do you show you are faithful to God?

[C] 1 Thes 3:12–4:2

1. What kind of heart should each of us have?
2. How can you conduct yourself so as to please God?

_____

_____

Gospel

[A] Mt 24:37–44

1. What does the coming of the Son of Man refer to?
2. What must you do to be prepared for Christ's coming?

[B] Mk 13:33–37

1. For what does Jesus tell us to watch?
2. How can you "be on guard" for his coming?

[C] Lk 21:25–28, 34–36

1. What is Jesus describing in this Gospel?
2. For what does he tell us to pray?

_____

_____

Second Reading

[A] 1 Pt 1:3–9

1. Why does God allow us to suffer sometimes?
2. What is the goal of our faith?

[B] 1 Jn 5:1–6

1. If we love God, whom else will we love?
2. What is the power that conquers the world? How can you "conquer the world" in your daily life?

[C] Rv 1:9–13, 17–18

1. John sees someone among the lampstands. Who is he and what does he call himself?
2. What does the Son of Man tell John to do about his visions?

_____

_____

Gospel *[A, B, C] Jn 20:19–31*

1. When Jesus appeared to his apostles on Easter Sunday night, what did he wish them? What gift or power did he give them?
2. What did Thomas say he had to do before he would believe Jesus was really present? What did Thomas say when Jesus appeared a week later?

_____

_____

✝ God's people prepared for the coming of Christ *in history*. Jesus comes to us every day *in mystery*—in the Eucharist, people, Scripture, and events. He will come again *in majesty* at the end of time to judge the living and the dead.

How can I prepare for his daily coming? for his final coming? Talk with Jesus—tell him how you plan to prepare for his comings; ask for his help.

Christmas—Mass at Midnight

First Reading *Is 9:1-6*

1. By what names do we call Jesus?
2. Christ's kingdom will be "forever peaceful." How can I be a peacemaker at home? with friends? in school?

Second Sunday of Easter

First Reading

[A] Acts 2:43-47
1. The brethren are the early Christians. To what activities did they devote themselves?
2. How did the believers feel about their way of life? How do you feel about your way of life as a follower of Christ?

[B] Acts 4:32-35
1. How did the early Christians share all things?
2. Would you like to live this way? Why? Why not?

[C] Acts 5:12-16
1. What signs and wonders did the apostles work?
2. How did the people show special respect for Peter? How do you show respect for Church leaders?

Responsorial Psalm *[A, B, C] Ps 118:2-4, 13-15, 22-24*
1. When was Jesus, the stone, rejected? When did he become the cornerstone?
2. What part of this psalm is most meaningful to you? How can you use it to help you this coming week?

Responsorial Psalm *Ps 96:1–3, 11–13*

1. How will Christ rule the world?
2. In what ways can I "tell his glory" to others?

_____

_____

Second Reading *Ti 2:11–14*

1. According to Paul, how should we live while we wait for the appearing of the glory of God?
2. Christ died to save us from evil. How do I show I am eager to do what is right?

_____

_____

Gospel *Lk 2:1–14*

1. Who were the first people to be told of the birth of the Savior? How were they told?
2. If Jesus were born today in our city, who do you think would be the first people told? Why?

_____

_____

✝ Tell Jesus you want to spread the good news of his coming by being a messenger of peace and justice, joy, and love. Ask him to show you how.

[B] Mt 1:12–15

1. Why did the Holy Spirit lead Jesus into the desert?
2. "Reform your lives and believe in the good news!" What do you feel you should change in your life?

_____

_____

✝ Each of us wants to be the kind of person Jesus wants, but it is hard to do right. The devil, people and things around us, and even we ourselves tempt us to do the easy or evil thing. Talk over with Jesus any problem you have doing what is right. Ask Jesus to help you fight evil and do what he expects of you.

6

First Sunday of Lent

First Reading

[A] Gn 2:7–9; 3:1–7

1. Why did Adam and Eve sin?

2. How did that first, or original, sin affect us?

[B] Gn 9:8–15

1. What did the rainbow God put in the sky represent?

2. What could rainbows mean in your life?

[C] Dt 26:4–10

1. Moses repeats some of the history of the chosen people. Why do you think he does this?

2. How does hearing about God's goodness to the chosen people strengthen your faith?

Responsorial Psalm

[A] Ps 51:3–6, 12–14, 17

1. With the psalmist we admit personal sin. What do we ask God to create in us?

2. How are we assured our sins are forgiven?

[B] Ps 25:4–9

1. What do we ask the Lord to teach us?

2. How can you "walk in his way" this week?

[C] Ps 91:1–2, 10–15

1. What is one thing that God, our refuge, will do, according to this psalm?

2. When have you experienced God's help in trouble?

Second Reading

[A] Rom 5:12–19 (or 17–19)

1. The sin of one man (Adam) caused all people to be condemned. What does the redeeming act of one man (Christ) do?

2. Jesus' obedience to the Father's will saved us. How can I know God's will for me?

[B] 1 Pt 3:18–22

1. Why did Christ die for our sins?

2. When are we cleansed of sin through his resurrection?

[C] Rom 10:8–13

1. What does St. Paul tell us to do to be saved?

2. *Confess* here means "to show" or "to give witness to." What are some ways you can give witness to Christ, or show him to others?

Gospel

[A] Mt 4:1–11 and [C] Lk 4:1–13

1. What is one thing the devil tempted Jesus to do? How can this be a temptation for us too?

2. Jesus answers the devil by quoting Scripture. Which quotation summarizes how we should live?